Manpower Policies for Youth

Edited by ELI E. COHEN and LOUISE KAPP

COLUMBIA UNIVERSITY PRESS

New York and London 1966

Eli E. Cohen is Executive Secretary, and Louise Kapp is
Director of Publications, of the National Committee on
Employment of Youth, a nonprofit, nongovernmental
research and consultative organization.

Manpower Policies for Youth

SELECTED PAPERS FROM

Manpower Policies for Youth: Priorities in Meeting

the Youth Employment Crisis

A SYMPOSIUM SPONSORED BY THE

NATIONAL COMMITTEE ON EMPLOYMENT OF YOUTH

IN WASHINGTON, D.C., SEPTEMBER 23–25, 1964

To the memory of Gertrude Folks Zimand

FOREWORD

by W. Willard Wirtz

WHEN the Symposium on Manpower Policies for Youth convened in Washington in September, 1964, I said that I considered the then general unconcern for youth—particularly those sixteen through twenty-one—Democracy's single, most serious default.

This conference did much to alter that situation.

The problem of employment for youth called for bold action, based on equally bold thinking. The papers presented then—particularly those here made available to the public—were certainly bold. I found their chief value lay in measuring the problem, not merely in terms of jobs for the young but in terms of education needs and the elimination of poverty and discrimination.

We can be grateful that many of the suggestions mulled over at the Symposium not only took root but have already born fruit.

I am also glad that a few did not. I refer to the alarm, expressed by some, that the involvement of government in manpower policies for youth posed more threat than promise.

At the time of the conference new government policies were already taking shape, with more on the way. Taking a look at the total employment picture today, I think we can be grateful for the innovative Federal programs which have resulted in approximately half the reduction in unemployment in 1965: the education, manpower training, vocational education, and antipoverty acts.

So far as youth is concerned, last year we were faced with the entrance of 650,000 more boys and girls sixteen through twenty-one into the labor force. At the same time, nearly 2½ million new jobs were created in the nonagricultural sector of the economy, 800,000 of them going to teenagers.

It was programs, as well as prosperity, that caused a decrease of 150,000 in the number of youthful unemployed. Many of those directly affected by our programs were the boys and girls who were least affected, in their employment opportunities, by the expansion of the economy.

At the end of 1965, about 150,000 boys and girls sixteen to twenty-one were working in the Neighborhood Youth Corps, which provides work for students from poor families, including many in school who could not otherwise stay there. Another 17,000 were participating in residential work-training programs in the Job Corps. And 100,000 college students, many of whom might otherwise have been unable to continue their studies, were benefiting from the work-study program which provides part-time work.

In over 100 different locations, the Department of Labor set up Youth Opportunity Centers—specifically to guide, counsel, and find employment for young people in need of these services.

During the summer of 1965, moreover, the Youth Opportunity Campaign helped stimulate at least 1 million new temporary summer jobs for boys and girls sixteen to twenty-one, enabling those youngsters to gain important work experience and earn needed wages.

This is quite a record.

The very magnificence of our accomplishments, however, makes our failures more acute, and leads us to return to the fertile ideas of this Symposium for continuing inspiration.

The unemployment rate for youths of sixteen to twenty-one has dropped from 14 to 12 percent—still far too high, and still four times the rate for adults. About a fourth of our unemployed are in this group, although they represent less than a tenth of the work force.

The postwar baby crop will continue coming of age, until by 1970 nearly half of the United States population will be under the age of twenty-five. The effect is already enormous, on our schools as well as on our labor force. Last year we had expected an increase of 215,000 boys and girls in college. It was 50 percent greater than that. Girls increased by 200,000, boys by 115,000. Perhaps 50,000 of the total reflects a decision of some boys to stay in school instead of going into military service. The rest represents the antipoverty program at work, civil rights maturing into civil results, and the great society coming true in people's lives.

College is one answer to job preparation, but it isn't the only answer, or the answer for all young people. Schools bear a heavy responsibility to broaden their scope. The democratic ideal is pressed too far when almost everyone is kept on the road to college despite the fact that fewer than half will get there.

Neither are "jobs for youth" the only answer. We should take little satisfaction in the increased employment figures for anybody under the age of twenty. The jobs these youngsters get are all too often ones that will later be done by machine.

Rather, we should orient the first twenty years of most American boys' and girls' lives toward training, perhaps in some cases a mixture of education and vocational training, with the emphasis on preparation. Not to forget preparation for leisure as well as for jobs—for work, but a shorter work life.

Another point. Why should the content of what children are

taught be dictated by what "the system" needs? We should, instead, be thinking about assuring every boy and girl the opportunity to develop to the full whatever may be his or her talents and capacities.

We have just started, beginning in late 1965, on a Human Resources Development Program—an individualized rather than institutionalized program to survey and register each young unemployed person, with the idea of tailoring our training to meet their specific needs.

So, if this Foreword takes a proud look backward, it has not forgotten the other direction. We have come a long way since the Symposium convened. And we have a long way to go in tailoring our manpower policies toward making people's lives as worth-while as they can be.

Manpower must mean the fuel power within people, not just what it takes to push the buttons.

ACKNOWLEDGMENTS

WE ARE indebted, first of all, to the Ford Foundation, which generously underwrote all of the basic costs of the Manpower Policies for Youth Symposium. Secondly our thanks go to Edward T. Chase, who originated the idea of the Symposium and helped to plan all of its details in his role as secretary to the Symposium's advisory committee. The advisory committee was as industrious as it was distinguished, and we are grateful to each member: James Dumpson, John Kenneth Galbraith, Nat Goldfinger, Mildred Jeffrey, Samuel V. Merrick, S. M. Miller, Daniel Patrick Moynihan, Howard J. Samuels, and Arthur M. Schlesinger, Jr. Finally, we wish to thank Marian Maury of Columbia University Press for her always helpful editorial assistance.

E.E.C.
L.K.

INTRODUCTION

ONE MIGHT expect to find these essays rusty, if not entirely dated. They stem, as Secretary Wirtz notes, from a symposium held by the National Committee on Employment of Youth in the autumn of 1964. At that time the Economic Opportunity Act had just been passed by Congress, but it would be several months before antipoverty programs would get under way. The U.S. role in Vietnam was still being publicly if unconvincingly portrayed as merely technical; the escalation that many were fearing had not yet begun. The economy was growing vigorously, experts said, but one of the thorniest debates was over what effect the tax cut that year would have on the unemployment rate, stuck for over six years at 5 percent or more. Not a few economists were beginning to despair that the nation would ever again achieve full employment, which they defined variously as a 3 or 4 percent unemployment rate.

Yet, two years and many relevant events later, the essays remain surprisingly, disturbingly apt. New material about changes in the economy and about the antipoverty program have been added by a number of contributors for the publication of this book. But in no case have they altered their original premises. Those premises vary widely, as do the fields from which the contributors come—government, business, labor, education, sociology, economics—but on one point they are unanimous: that the obstinate trend of out-of-school, out-of-work, out-of-hope young people will not be broken by economic growth alone, nor, vital though they may be at present, by temporary crash programs.

The statistics bear out this view. Along with gains in adult employment, the number of working youths soared last year. So, however, did the number seeking work. By January, 1966, with the overall jobless rate at last down to 4 percent, with well advertised labor shortages remaining, with an accelerated draft reducing the youth labor force, with Neighborhood Youth Corps, Job Corps, and other antipoverty programs absorbing hundreds of thousands of youths, the statisticians still found one out of every eight young people looking for work without luck, one out of four among Negro youths. And that did not include a sizable proportion of young people not counted in the unemployment statistics because they were not actively looking for work; they had given up trying.

Inside and outside of government, there is now only minor disagreement that (barring an even larger war) low income youths will continue to experience grave problems in finding work unless long-range policies in their behalf are found and applied. If nothing else, the prospect of the vast wave of youths coming of working age in the years immediately ahead —with half of the population under 25 by 1970—has startled even the most soporific among us. The fact that Negroes, who suffer the most obstacles, will constitute a disproportionate share of the increase is not being overlooked either. White America has yet to acknowledge its debt to the Negro protest movement for forcing attention to the problems of poverty afflicting whites and blacks alike—problems which affect, numerically, an increasing number of whites. In the related case of youth unemployment, the debt runs equally high.

But precisely what policies are needed? How can they be put into action? And what is the price? Here is where agreement ends. An exploration of why so many low-income youths are today unemployed and underemployed is forbiddingly like a discussion of the world-and-what-it-contains. The subject embraces nearly everything: the very different kinds of young people involved, the impact of poverty and discrimination, the role of education and training, the quantity and quality of available work, the practices and policies toward youth of business and labor, the overall economy, the draft, automation, the war on poverty, and more.

The essays that follow are not that encyclopedic, but they necessarily cover quite a bit of ground. They are concerned with three broad areas: preparation for work, manpower utilization, and job creation. Each area in reality interconnects with the others, and one of the frequent pleas in these papers is that public policies in the three areas must also begin to interconnect.

Hence, in suggesting improved ways of preparing youth for employment, Clarence Senior, Nat Hentoff, S. M. Miller, and Marcia K. Freedman all add the caveat that education without social change, training without suitable jobs, are at best palliatives, at worst a hoax.

A good many contributors—among them Ivar Berg, Leon H. Keyserling, Eli Ginzberg, and John H. Rubel—question the most widely held assumption about youth unemployment today: that it is primarily caused by inadequate education. Several examples are given to show how people with little or no education can be trained to fill highly technical jobs as ably as more educated workers. In demanding higher educational qualifications than jobs may actually require, employers are not only in danger of shortchanging themselves and thousands of potentially valuable workers, but, says Ivar Berg, they may also be seriously "distorting the manpower picture and contributing to significant misallocation in the distribution and utilization of manpower."

Sheer ignorance of job vacancies distorts the manpower picture further. Calling for measures to fully develop the U.S. Employment Service into a national labor market exchange, Senator Joseph S. Clark and Edward T. Chase recommend giving employers tax incentives to induce them to list all of their vacancies.

Tax incentives are also urged by several contributors to encourage employers to hire unskilled youth, a proposal that one spokesman from business, Howard J. Samuels, while not ruling out, clearly does not relish. In his view, the unemployed-because-uneducated equation still holds and new policies must not jeopardize the first concern of business: productivity and profits.

Moreover, Mr. Samuels predicts, because of advancing labor-displacing technology in private industry, the job future for youths lies largely in the public sector. Assuming, of course, that investment in public services expands as quickly and on the scale that contributors such as Leon H. Keyserling propose. A year ago that seemed not an impossible hope. Today, with the sleep of public officials jarred by nightmares of runaway inflation, there is ample room for doubt.

According to Eli Ginzberg, it is always easier for government to take action when there is a massive number of unemployed, as there was in the Depression of the 1930s, because "in a crisis it need not be concerned with costs." The great difficulty, he says, is in finding measures that will not threaten the economy when the vast majority of people are employed. If they are not found, the result would be the most bizarre irony of all—that precisely because we have reached unprecedented prosperity and high employment, we cannot justify spending on behalf of those left behind. We would first have to wait for the predictions of Ben B. Seligman and W. H. Ferry to come true, for automation and cybernation to sweep out the bulk of the labor force, or, at least, for another recession.

We surely have more options than that. As Robert L. Heilbroner notes in his summary of the symposium's proceedings, whether one is apocalyptic or optimistic about the future, the hard question must still be asked: what steps do we take next? And that is what these essays seek to find out.

ELI E. COHEN AND LOUISE KAPP

NATIONAL COMMITTEE ON

EMPLOYMENT OF YOUTH

New York, N.Y.
July, 1966

CONTENTS

Manpower Policies for Youth

NEW APPROACHES TO FINANCING
EDUCATION AND TRAINING

by Clarence Senior

Clarence Senior is a member of the Board of Education of the City of New York, and Professor of Sociology at Brooklyn College. He belongs to numerous civic and professional organizations, and has written widely in the fields of education, housing, intergroup relations, inter-American affairs, land reform, population problems, and sociology. Two of his recent books are *Our Citizens from the Caribbean* and *The Puerto Ricans: Strangers—Then Neighbors*.

MAY I start by a fervent "amen" to those who have said that there must be significant social changes before our society will be playing fair with our youth—or with any of its working citizens for that matter. We know from innumerable studies that aspiration levels are intimately related to the realities of economic opportunities. And we know that the concentration only on achieving a higher income can be self-defeating. Without more of a sense of purpose in work and in life as a whole, without greater chances for all persons to achieve a sense of dignity and personal worth, we will continue to have a society in which frustrations and aggressions multiply. We will not achieve a better society by using outworn slogans and hoary clichés; it should be part of the duties of the schools to help students learn that just as they and their families must plan for the future, so must society. The programs that are necessary to secure enough education and training, and of the proper types, will require more of an investment than we have yet indicated the will to make. Let me make it clear that I do not consider more money as anything more than a *necessary* requisite to the education we need; it is not *sufficient*. Education can and must change, and many interested professionals and laymen are now addressing themselves to the elements needing improvement.

Our democratic commitment to equal opportunity for *all* means a commitment to the education of all to the limit of their abilities. It requires a direct and sustained attack on the concept that has cursed our Western culture since the days of the Greek philosophers, writing in the luxury made possible by slavery and teaching that some men were born to rule and others to be ruled. This doctrine has been particularly vicious in our own country since the apologists for slavery discovered that the Negro was doomed to an inferior existence because Ham found his father "drunk and disorderly," as the police blotter might say nowadays.[1]

We have, since the turn of the century, increased the number of pupils in our public school system from 15,503,110 to 36,087,000. This means from 72 percent of the five- to seventeen-year-olds in 1900 to 82 percent in 1960. (And the number of private school students has risen from 1,351,722 to 5,674,943.) We have lengthened the school year from an average of 144 days in 1900 to 178 days sixty years later. High school graduates have increased from 6 percent of the population to 37 percent. In 1960 we had 2,008 institutions of higher education, compared with 977 in 1900. They graduated 392,-440 students in 1960, compared with 27,410 in 1900.

We have increased our expenditures for public day schools about seventy times in the six decades: from $214,965,000 to $14,991,000,000. Current expenditures per pupil in average

---

[1] For a brilliant exposition of how the Negro was systematically robbed of his rights and his dignity as a human being, see Stanley M. Elkins, *Slavery: a Problem in American Institutional and Intellectual Life* (New York, Grosset's Universal Library, 1963).

daily attendance rose from $16.67 to $472.17, or twenty-eight times, in the sixty years.[2] Yet on every hand we find shortages of classrooms and teachers leading to short-time instruction, double sessions, oversized classes, and overworked and under-paid teachers, many of whom are inadequately trained. Obso-lescent schools still are in use in spite of leaking roofs, infesta-tion with rats and vermin, inadequate toilets, and lack of mod-ern equipment. Even the good buildings are not used on a year-round basis, day and night, as they should be.

Textbooks are out of date in many schools, and quite gener-ally there are neither sufficient texts nor library books.

Guidance counselors should be available for every 250 to 300 students, but even our best systems seldom achieve that aver-age.

PROSPECTS FOR THE NEAR FUTURE

We have been through a decade of rapid growth in the school-age population and in school enrollments. During this period persons registered, by year and by level, numbered:

	Total	Elementary, including Kindergarten	High School	Higher Education
1950	30,276,000	21,406,000	6,656,000	2,214,000
1955	37,426,000	27,086,000	7,961,000	2,379,000
1960	46,259,000	32,441,000	10,249,000	3,570,000

In what would seem to be a most realistic projection for the next decades, the Census Bureau foresees the following num-bers: [3]

[2] Data from *Historical Statistics of the United States: Colonial Times to 1957,* and *Statistical Abstract of the United States, 1963* (Washington, Government Printing Office, 1960 and 1963).

[3] *Statistical Abstract, 1963,* p. 118. See also Donald J. Bogue, "Population

	Total	Elementary, including Kindergarten	High School	Higher Education
1965	54,360,000	35,755,000	13,226,000	6,000,000
1970	60,344,000	38,430,000	14,894,000	8,000,000
1975	66,721,000	42,411,000	15,985,000	10,000,000
1980	75,102,000	48,696,000	17,388,000	12,000,000

These figures give an idea of how great will be the demand for buildings, teachers, teachers' aides, teacher-training facilities, new equipment, new text and library books, etc., in the next few years.

There are two other major factors which will cost more money. One is experimentation. Industry and the Federal government now spend huge sums of money annually in trying out new ideas and searching for more effective ways of conducting their work. The 1961–62 fiscal year saw $14,740 million spent for "research and development" in the United States. The Federal government supplied $9,650 million; industry, $4,705 million; colleges and universities, $230 million; and other nonprofit organizations, $155 million. Little of this went to research in the fields most relevant to public education.

The second is an extremely important and relatively new task which is increasingly being assumed by the more advanced school systems. It must be extended to all. This is the assumption of more responsibility for successfully preparing the student to earn a living, *and* helping to place him even if this must be done several times before he finds the correct start for his occupational career. I agree with Dr. James B. Conant when, after discussing the need for greater cooperation among the schools, employers, labor unions, employment agencies,

Growth in the United States," *Population Bulletin* (Washington, Population Reference Bureau), XX, No. 1 (Feb. 1964), 5–27. His figures are used for the high school estimates.

and social agencies, he concludes that "guidance officers, especially in the large cities, ought to be given the responsibility for following the post-high school careers of youth from the time they leave school until they are twenty-one years of age." [4]

We now have a virtual consensus among labor economists and employment counselors that the idea of training for a specific set of occupational skills may well be outmoded and that a worker may have to be retrained several times during his economically productive life span. At the very least, we know the industries and occupations in which employment is declining and those in which it is likely to increase. [5]

What we really need, of course, is an educational system which will prepare persons for widespread social, economic, and political change and for the idea that man must learn how to plan and direct his own future.

HOW ARE WE TO FINANCE THE SCHOOLS
OF THE FUTURE?

There is, obviously, no simple solution to adequate financing of schools, which must expand their activities and play a key role in building a society that will help bring our democratic ideals to fruition in all aspects of life. The very process of undertaking such a formidable task alienates some persons who will attempt to sabotage the public school system. (We in New York City could speak at length on this aspect since a recent anti-integration boycott cost our system $1,600,000 in state aid!)

One approach to an answer to our question is to examine the

[4] James B. Conant, *Slums and Suburbs* (New York, McGraw-Hill, 1961), p. 41.
[5] For example, see the succinct report by Harold Goldstein, "The Economic Setting for Vocational Guidance," a reprint from *Occupational Outlook Quarterly*, VII, No. 3 (Sept. 1963).

wide variation in school support which now prevails, between
states and within states.

Let us look first at several measures of ability to support
education. Per capita personal income is certainly one of them.
We find that in 1962 the state averages ranged from $3,278 for
Nevada to $1,285 for Mississippi. The national average was
$2,366, with seventeen states above the average and thirty-
three below it.[6] Seven states were at least 20 percent above the
national average: Nevada, 138 percent; Delaware, 131 percent;
Connecticut, 131 percent; New York, 124 percent; California,
122 percent; New Jersey, 122 percent; Illinois, 120 percent.
Mississippi was 54 percent. But the number of children of
school age (five to seventeen) varies greatly from state to state,
with the largest proportions found in exactly those states which
most need education. The personal income per child in this age
group varies from $13,556 in Nevada to Mississippi's $4,479.
The United States average is $9,429, with thirty-five states be-
low it.

Tax revenues of state and local governments used for support of public elementary and secondary schools also range
widely. For the nation as a whole local governments supply
56.4 percent of the school budgets, state governments 40.1. The
remaining 3.5 percent comes from the Federal government.
The amount of taxes collected for all purposes and specifically
for schools also fluctuates substantially from state to state, both
in absolute terms and relative to personal income. New York
heads the list as collector of the highest tax per capita: $309.05
in 1962, but it dropped to ninth place in percentage of personal
income (10.6 percent). The national average for per capita
taxes was $223.46; proportionate to personal income, 9.4 per-

[6] These and the following data are from Research Report, 1964-R1, *Rank-
ings of the States, 1964* (Washington, National Education Association, 1964).

cent. The lowest collector was Alabama, with $131.66; its nearest companions were South Carolina, Arkansas, and Mississippi. But Mississippi, which ranked forty-seventh in total per capita collections, ranked fourth in the percentage scale, with 11 percent. It was preceded by Louisiana and Vermont, with 11.5; and Minnesota, 11.2.

Next we come to one of the critical blocks to flexibility in the tax structure: the property tax. One tax authority, George W. Mitchell, states that "probably no tax form in modern fiscal times is as poorly managed as the property tax." [7] An illustration of a major weakness of the property tax is the wide spread in assessment practices, with the national average at 29 percent of market value but with Rhode Island assessing at 67.6 percent and South Carolina at 5.4 percent! Mitchell also indicts it for interfering with urban redevelopment and doing "little to discourage particular private investment decisions resulting in congestion and other heavy community costs." [8] The proportion of state and local taxes originating in the property tax would appear to be a helpful index to the flexibility of such governmental tax income. For the United States as a whole, 45.9 percent of all local and state tax revenues comes from the property tax, with twenty-four states above that average. The range is from Nebraska with 70.3 percent, to Hawaii with 16 percent. In the State of New York the proportion is 43.9 percent.

Ability to pay for education of course is not equivalent to *willingness* to pay! This is illustrated by the list of states ranked by total public school revenue receipts as a proportion of personal income. The national average is 4.3 percent. The

[7] George W. Mitchell, quoted in Dick Netzer, "The Property Tax and Alternatives in Urban Development," *Papers and Proceedings of the Regional Science Association,* XI (1962), 191–200.
[8] *Ibid.,* p. 198.

top ten states are Utah, 5.8 percent; New Mexico and Louisiana, 5.4 percent; Alaska, Mississippi, Oregon, Wyoming, and Minnesota, all with 5.3 percent; Montana, 5.2 percent; and Arizona, 5.1 percent. The bottom ten include another strange assortment: Kentucky, New Jersey, and Maryland, with 3.8 percent; Connecticut and Illinois, 3.7 percent; Nebraska, 3.6 percent; New Hampshire and Rhode Island, 3.5 percent; Missouri, 3.4 percent; Nevada, 3.4 percent; and Massachusetts, 2.8 percent.

The actual receipts per pupil in average daily attendance also differ widely, the average for the United States being $541. New York tops the list with $826. Alabama is in fiftieth place, with $304. Only nineteen states rank above the national average.

Finally, where does the Federal government fit into the school revenue picture? We have seen that the national average is a contribution of 3.5 percent to public elementary and secondary schools. There is an extremely wide range here: Alaska and Hawaii receive 24.1 percent and 10.1 percent, respectively. New York is fiftieth, with 1.7 percent. Twenty-nine states rank above the national average.

One more set of interstate comparisons must be made in passing: the per capita state and local governmental expenditures for higher education in 1962. California ranks first, with $45.14; Massachusetts last, with $6.47. Its closest neighbors are Pennsylvania, $8.48; Connecticut, $10.92; and New York, in forty-seventh place with $12.46. The United States average is $21.71. Perhaps the New York State government and Chamber of Commerce should examine these figures carefully when discussing why California is outstripping New York in growth of wealth and population!

Let us look more closely at New York State as an example of

the difficulties faced in equitably allocating state funds. The Public Education Association points out that:

Since the days of Governor Smith, New Yorkers generally have accepted the principle that all of the children of the State are enti-tled to at least a minimum opportunity for education and that wealthier communities should be taxed to guarantee that this mini-mum will be provided even in the poorer communities. The present law requires the State to pay 49 percent of the school costs in dis-tricts of average financial resources—up to a maximum operating expenditure of $500 per pupil. The wealthier communities receive less than 49 percent, and poorer districts receive a proportionately larger percentage of state aid.[9]

Actually, New York City received only 31.7 percent of its 1963–64 operating budget of $839,490,653 from the State.[10]

While the general principle stated above seems reasonable, two major items make it discriminatory against the larger school systems. First, school costs generally increase greater than proportionately with an increase in city size. Site acquisi-tion costs, for example, averaged $1,355 for New York's non-city school districts, but Syracuse sites cost $34,695 and those in New York City $206,138.

In addition, the larger cities serve more academic and voca-tional high school students than do most towns and smaller cities. The New York City 1962–63 instruction budget per pupil rose as follows:

Elementary Schools	$ 666.72
Junior High Schools	753.99
Academic High Schools	796.98
Vocational High Schools	1,196.14

[9] *A Citizen's Guide to the New York City Public Schools and Colleges.* (New York, Public Education Association, 1963), p. 24.
[10] *Facts and Figures, 1963–64* (New York, Board of Education, 1964).

There were, in addition, in 1963, the following specialized classes, each of which is more costly than regular classes, and most of which are not generally found in smaller systems: health conservation, 340; hospital and convalescent homes, 154; sight conservation, 99; Braille, 23; deaf, 65; remand centers and shelters, 377; aphasic, 23; and classes for children with retarded mental development, 841. Pupils in these classes numbered 31,600. Home instruction is provided for 1,775 pupils by 327 itinerant teachers.

New York City's kindergarten to twelfth grade enrollment comprises 35 percent of the State's elementary and secondary rolls, but it accounts for 72 percent of all the vocational, trade, and technical pupils in the State and for 50.5 percent of all the children in classes for the handicapped.[11]

Second, municipal overhead costs for non-school purposes —fire and police protection, water supply, sanitation, etc.—are much higher the larger the city.[12]

The Public Education Association study points out that wide variation in assessment practices in New York State have made a special "equalization" formula necessary to correct inequities. The desperate situation of the Detroit schools a few years ago led to the appointment of a Citizens Advisory Committee on School Needs. Its conclusion on state aid sounds familiar:

Increased funds from state sources cannot be anticipated with any certainty for the next five-year period. In the allocation of state funds there are many factors which place the school district of the City of Detroit at a distinct disadvantage in comparison with other school districts. Wide discrepancies in assessing procedures throughout the state must be corrected if the distribution of state aid is to

[11] *The Challenge of Financing Public Schools in Great Cities.* (Chicago, Research Council of the Great Cities Program for School Improvement, 1964), Table 4.

[12] Illustrations of this for central city and outlying areas of metropolitan areas are given in Harvey E. Brazer, *Some Fiscal Implications of Metropolitanism* (Washington, The Brookings Institution, 1962).

be on a more equitable basis. The formula for the distribution of funds now in effect, and those proposals which are contemplated by legislators, show no significant improvements for Detroit. Efforts to improve assessment practices in this state and to arrive at a more equitable formula for the distribution of state aid must be continued in the years ahead.[13]

NEW APPROACHES

First, it would seem obvious that administration of the property tax can be improved, strengthened, and made more equitable.

Second, some cities appear to have come close to the point of diminishing returns, since central city property values are quite generally falling. Unless urban renewal and related programs succeed in stemming the tide of outward movement to the suburbs as families climb the economic ladder (and therefore can afford to pay more taxes), the probabilities are that taxable assessed valuations per pupil will fall in all the bigger cities, as they did in ten of the fourteen largest cities during a recent five-year period.[14] Again, the fate of the schools is linked with the health of the cities and of the economy as a whole. Taxes on other than real property can be levied with less resistance during times of "prosperity" than when economic conditions are bad.

Third, state income taxes, with rebates to cities, are now being discussed in a number of jurisdictions. They also would be somewhat easier to levy during prosperous times.

FEDERAL AID

Next we come to the controversial question of Federal aid. There should, if we were logical, be no objection to such aid. It

[13] *Findings and Recommendations* (Detroit, Citizens Advisory Committee on School Needs, 1958), p. 323.
[14] *The Challenge of Financing Public Schools in Great Cities,* Table 8.

should be firmly based on the economic, social, and political reality of "one nation, indivisible," but to many citizens this is a slogan and not a living reality. One of our presidential candidates, for example, said that:

The government must begin to withdraw from a whole series of programs that are outside its constitution mandate—from social welfare programs, education . . . and all the other activities that can be better proffered by lower levels of government or by private institutions or by individuals.[15]

On the other hand, we have a growing weight of testimony regarding how crucial education has been, and is, in increasing the real wealth and the productivity of our "human resources." It was seen abroad as early as Adam Smith, and in this country in 1906 by the conservative economist Irving Fisher, in his *Nature of Capital and Income*. More recently it has been worked out with great care by such economists as Theodore W. Schultz, Gary S. Becker, Solomon Fabricant, H. P. Miller, and John Kenneth Galbraith. Schultz and Galbraith especially have taken up the cudgels against "our failure to invest in people," to quote the latter, or our "shying away from investment in man," as Schultz puts it.[16]

The widespread internal migration of our people means that our big city school systems inherit the handicaps of the citizens born and raised in areas where schooling is horribly inadequate. New York City's schools, for example, received 39,490 students from other communities during 1962–63. Foreign countries were the source of 6,250, Puerto Rico and the West Indies, 11,173, and other New York State communities, 5,385.

[15] Barry M. Goldwater, *Conscience of a Conservative* (Shepherdsville, Ky., Victor Publishing Co., 1960), p. 69.
[16] See Theodore W. Schultz, "Investment in Human Capital," *American Economic Review*, LI, No. 1 (March, 1961), pp. 1–17, for argument and bibliography; and John Kenneth Galbraith, *The Affluent Society* (Boston, Houghton Mifflin, 1958), p. 332.

Ten Middle and South Atlantic states supplied 10,857. Six of these ten states were above the national average in illiteracy and seven of the ten were above it in selective service registrants failing the preinduction mental test. Schools of cities in the North Central states experience the same kind of difficulty with Southerners, both white and Negro, plus some Indians and Mexican-Americans. And the Rocky Mountain and Pacific Coast states also receive sizable numbers of the same ethnic groups.

The extent of internal migration is little realized. One measure—which understates the case—showed 44,263,882 persons in 1960 living in a state different from that in which they had been born, or 24.9 percent of the national population. (In 1850 the percentage was 21.3!) Persons born in the South and living in the North numbered 6,569,567; born in the North but living in the South, 4,546,921; born east of the Mississippi River but living west of it, 7,544,295; born west but living east, 3,571,970.

Even more striking are the annual data on persons moving and migrating. Since records have been kept, some 30 to 35 million persons have moved their homes each year. Those who move within the same county number about 20 million; another 5 million move across county lines but within the same state; and still another 5 million move across state lines. Invariably, those who move between noncontiguous states outnumber those who move across only one state border. Economists find such mobility essential to the prosperity of the country. The Federal government recognized that many of these moves were in response to demands of our war economy, which gave rise to aid to "impacted areas" of World War II days. Public Laws 815 and 874 continue to cover areas in which the impact of Federal employment on local school facilities is so great as to require Federal aid to local school systems.

Up until 1961, Federal assistance to education was limited to relatively restricted geographical or functional areas. Except for the early land grants in aid of schools, the chief beneficiaries were the fields related to agricultural, home economics, and distributive occupations, plus the veterans' "bill of rights." Federal funds as a factor in the regular income of public elementary and secondary schools first appeared in the official government reports in 1918, when they amounted to $1,669,000. Twenty years later, the sum had risen to $26,535,000. By 1948 the total was still only $120 million, but by 1958 it had risen to $496 million and by 1960 to $652 million. It still supplied only 4.4 percent of total educational expenditures in the nation.

The National Defense Education Act of 1958 set forth a program to improve teaching, especially in the sciences, mathematics, and foreign languages. Increasing "pockets" of prolonged and sustained high unemployment gave rise to the Area Redevelopment Act (ARA) in 1961. It was followed in March, 1962 by the Manpower Development and Training Act (MDTA), and that was followed a few months later by the Trade Expansion Act. All four provided funds, although inadequate, for training or retraining of carefully circumscribed categories of workers. By 1963, Federal government expenditures for education had risen to $1,605 million, or more than double the 1960 figure of $652 million. In addition, $111 million was made available that year for construction of school plants.[17]

The Economic Opportunity Act of 1964, signed on August 20, broadened the scope of Federal support to various educational activities. Four of the six major titles provide programs

[17] *New Directions in Health, Education and Welfare* (Washington, Health, Education and Welfare, 1963), p. 88.

and funds for some form of education. The Office of Economic Opportunity operates the Job Corps, the program for Volunteers in Service to America (VISTA), a community action program, and special programs, including education, for migrant workers. In addition, it distributes funds, for operating several programs authorized under the Act, to existing agencies: the Department of Labor for work-training programs; the Department of Health, Education and Welfare for work-study programs, adult basic education, and community work and training programs for welfare recipients; the Department of Agriculture for special rural antipoverty programs; and the Small Business Administration for loans to small business.

Although the funds are grossly inadequate for the task which must be accomplished, it may well be that a pattern has been set which can be used to establish a viable and adequate program.

ADDITIONAL FINANCIAL AID

There are two more sources of funds for education: private foundations and private business. The former, numbering 5,202, each with assets of $1 million or more, gave some $257 million annually for education in 1957 and 1958. The 154 largest, each with assets of $10 million or more, gave $212 million in 1960. Some of the experimental work being done in education is foundation-financed.[18]

On-the-job training is of two major types of apprenticeship; it is usually conducted by unions alone, but sometimes jointly by unions and employers. The 1960 census listed 80,316 men and 2,221 women as apprentices. This, of course, is only a drop in the sea of the operatives and kindred workers sector of the labor force, which numbered 11,897,501. Schultz points out

[18] *Statistical Abstract, 1963,* p. 315.

that "apprenticeship had all but disappeared, partly because it is inefficient and partly because schools now perform many of its functions." [19] But, although he also points out that "surprisingly little is known about on-the-job training in modern industry," he quotes one study that places the amount invested in such training at about equal to the amount spent on formal education. A Chase Manhattan Bank survey in 1962 led to an estimate that "some $17 billion of resources will be devoted to these activities this year. That's an additional $1 for every $3 which goes for education in our school system, including public and private, elementary and secondary schools and colleges." The survey concludes that:

Altogether, the value of the on-the-job training which has been accumulated by all of the men now in the labor force runs to approximately $450 billion, and this investment is growing at a rate of 5½ per cent per annum. This is 70 per cent as large as the estimated $650 billion which was invested in the formal education of those now working, and this investment has been growing 4 per cent a year. Both forms of investment in education have so increased the output of the economy—and the income of those educated—as to equal a return on investment of about 10 per cent.[20]

THE TWO CHALLENGES

Francis Keppel, the United States Commissioner of Education and former Dean of the Graduate School of Education, Harvard University, after stressing the critical need for greater investment in education, remarked that "the traditional content of both general education and occupational training at all levels is obsolescent." So, as we raise more money we must also revise the curriculum and raise educational standards. We can do both, if we will!

[19] Schultz, p. 10.
[20] "Education by Business," *Chase Manhattan Bulletin*, Nov.–Dec., 1962.

WHOSE EXISTENTIAL CRISIS?

by Nat Hentoff

Nat Hentoff is a writer on the staff of *The New Yorker*, a contributor to other publications, and the author of works of fiction and nonfiction. His latest nonfiction book is *The New Equality*, and his latest novel is *Call the Keeper*.

"WHAT we would like from you," I was told by way of orientation for this panel, "are your thoughts on 'the existential crisis in youth motivation.' What we mean by this is the problem of alienation—from school and work, from social institutions and middle-class values, etc., that dissuade the young from seeking education or employment or in fact from making any commitment to the larger society."

From my experiences with those who are called "disadvantaged" or "culturally deprived" youngsters, I would begin by pointing out that increasingly, acceleratingly, the core of this "existential crisis in youth motivation" is that these youngsters have been lied to all their lives—and they know it.

The Secretary of Labor has told of stopping a teenager in Harlem this past spring and asking him if he was looking for a job. The boy's answer was, "Why?"

That answer, I submit, was a healthy reaction. I would think it meant: "I've stopped letting myself be conned. I have eyes. I see what jobs are available to the adults in the ghetto. I *know* the lousy schooling I've had. Where am I supposed to look? And to put it where it is, *why* should I think things will change? Nobody out there gives a damn about me."

It's a healthy answer because it represents visceral as well as intellectual disgust at evasion—at the evasive hypocrisy of the middle-class majority and at his own self-evasion of reality which, I'm sure, has caused that youngster all kinds and shades of pain in the past each time he has been forced to recognize that "they" indeed did not give a damn about him out there— nor did "they" give a damn about him in the ghetto when they came in as teachers, as store owners, as cops.

Similarly, there are many cases in which the decision to drop out of school is an indication that some healthy resiliency is left in a youngster. A youngster who has been constricted and flattened all his school life by being caught in the vise of the pernicious track systems (with their morally and pedagogically indefensible "homogeneous" classes) winds up in a high school context in which he is either regarded as serving the terminal years of a sentence or is being "instructed" in vocational skills that were obsolete when he was in grammar school. Furthermore, because he has been allowed and expected to fail to develop adequate reading skills, along with the other basic tools for survival in even a pre-cybernated economy, he is embarrassed in a classroom. Why should he stay in a situation in which he feels the fool, in which the teachers regard him as a fool, and his parents already see themselves—as they are now—in him? If he has any life left, he cuts out, and tries to make it in the streets.

He won't make it. And the youngster in Harlem who spoke truth to the power of Secretary of Labor Wirtz also won't make it. So, though their reactions—in asking "Why?" or in leaving school—are healthy, it is a transitory health that is not likely to prevent their becoming full-fledged, lifetime members of the underclass.

I have begun this way because it is essential to recognize— viscerally as well as intellectually—that when we talk of these youngsters as being alienated, we so often use the passive form of the verb. Out of our complicity in the national guilt perhaps? Let me, for example, rephrase the orientation that was given me for this panel: "The problem is the degree to which *we* in the majority have alienated so many of the young from school and work, from social institutions and middle-class values. What have been *our* motivations—the motivations of that larger society—in allowing the ghettos to grow, in allowing the 'alienated' youngsters to increase?"

Until those who are concerned with this crisis, moreover, can actually engage in role reversal, can project themselves to some extent into the young of the underclass, nothing durable or basic is going to happen. Quite aside, for the moment, from the impossibility of finding meaningful work—as work is now defined—for masses of the undereducated young in a precipitously cybernated economy, how are you going to bring these youngsters into the "larger society" and into a commitment to "middle-class values" without also telling them that you know the larger society is in many ways sicker than they are and that so large a proportion of those middle-class values are false?

I say again that these youngsters have been lied to all their lives—about the "open society," about the "equality" of their education, about their own potential. The one hopeful thing about their present alienation is that, for the most part, they are trying very hard to avoid believing any more lies. If we feel there are some middle-class values worth preserving and worth passing on—if we feel the larger society has some viability left and can become the kind or quality of society that Robert Theobald and Gerard Piel, among others, have quite logically envisioned, we cannot convince the young in the underclass to commit themselves to that kind of future unless we can also convince them we respect them *now* by telling them what's wrong with the present.

Motivation does not begin with pedagogical techniques, or with love, or with bleak prophecies about the fate in the future of the undereducated man. It begins with respect—truth telling respect for the youngsters you're trying to reach. And that respect is in very short supply among those members of the "larger society" whom these young people meet.

Let me be specific. I have spent much of a year researching Mobilization for Youth on New York's Lower East Side. It became apparent to me soon after I began that the key division of Mobilization was not the World of Work or the homemaker service or even the attempts to change curricula in the local schools and to get teachers to break through their middle-class myopia so that they could see and *feel* the identities of the children. The key division was that section of Mobilization which was trying to reach the disaffiliated, young and older, in the community and to get them to organize themselves to work for change in the community, to realize their own potential for power and dignity. There were many routes toward this goal —rent strikes, protesting prejudice and inferior materials in Lower East Side schools, voter registration, etc.

After that year, I decided to wait for yet another year before I returned to Mobilization. The reason was that not enough had been happening. There had been stirrings toward self-action, but they were few and too often inchoate. A few weeks after I made my decision, all hell broke loose. The City's nurturer of Senator Joseph McCarthy's legacy, the *Daily News*, headlined the alleged presence of alleged Communists in Mobilization. Then there were the real charges—Mobilization had been involved in "irresponsible" social action, encouraging rent strikes, school boycotts, and the like.

New York City officials, predictably, caved in instantly. Federal figures of prominence with direct responsibility for Mobilization were hardly conspicuous in the speed or forthrightness of their public support of Mobilization's philosophy—a philosophy that clearly is not understood by most of the citizenry, right, left, or middle. That philosophy is, in part: disaffiliation ends when active commitment to the possibility of change in one's way of life begins. Not a word, moreover, from the then Attorney General in whose province Mobilization partly falls. What this official cowardice and apathy mean for the future of community organization in Mobilization is that Mobilization is going to run scared until it runs out.

Even though very little happened to change the distribution of power in the Lower East Side during Mobilization's active period of community organization, there were changes in what could be called "motivation" among some of the resident young. At first suspicious that Mobilization's crew was just another safari of welfare-worker colonialists sent into the jungles of the poor, some of these youngsters really came to believe after a while that there *were* people in Mobilization who did give a damn about them. That there were those in Mobilization who were almost as angry at the landlords of the poor as the poor were—who were willing, moreover, to help them get *at* those landlords. That there were those in Mobilization who knew, just as these kids did, that some of the teachers in the public schools called Puerto Ricans "bean eaters" and told Negro and Puerto Rican mothers that they should be grateful that the City of New York was taking any time at all in the "impossible" task of educating their youngsters. That there were those in Mobilization who not only knew who those teachers were but encouraged a group of local mothers to take action against them. The action was largely ineffectual, but at least there had been enough action to make those teachers and some equally offensive principals uncomfortable and aware that they might not be able to keep getting away with psycho-genicide indefinitely.

Now the youngsters on the Lower East Side who were reached—many of them, anyway—see Mobilization as having been yet another con game. This time, to be sure, some of the people in the "new establishment" itself also got conned. I mean the more believable workers in Mobilization. But at base I expect that the consensus on the Lower East Side has turned out to be what it's always been. You can't trust the emissaries of that larger society. Because they're liars. They may want to "help" you but they sure as hell don't want you to help yourself through getting some of what they have—power. Or, when some outsiders do want to join in *that* way, the money behind them is soon used as a club to "straighten" them out.

I have been emphasizing all this because I think it absurd to talk about motivating the young to continue in school, to seek work, to make a commitment to "the larger society" without being thoroughly clear—to oneself as well as to them—about the basic forces aligned against their breaking out of where they are. And hypocrisy is a major one. *They* know it, and to begin to communicate with them, you have to make them aware *you* know it too.

The danger of such programs as the U.S. Employment Service's Youth Opportunity Centers and the Job Corps—and others of this nascent and so tiny war on poverty—is not only that they can reach comparatively few of the drifting, young underclass but that they will serve as a conscience-soothing substitute for the more radical changes in the society which have to take place if the young are to have any real reason to be motivated toward full-scale participation in the society. It's been said so often that it's become a dulling litany, but it must be pointed out again that we are not going to approach this problem of motivation seriously unless we simultaneously work to get the billions of dollars needed to build schools, hire more teachers so that there will be much smaller classes, train teachers who know the strengths as well as the liabilities of the "culturally deprived," build educational parks so that real citywide integration can take place, and get rid of that damn track system which kills motivation in so many youngsters before they're out of elementary school.

We're not going to create reasons for youngsters to continue in school—even if the schools are worth going to—until we also make it possible for them to have jobs when they get out. And that means many more billions of dollars for all kinds of essential expenditures in public works, transportation, hospitals, conservation, etc. All of you here know the list. That's become a litany too. And even then, as Robert Theobald keeps telling anyone who will listen, there won't be enough jobs. Therefore, people should be *paid* for going to school. That is meaningful work. People should be *paid* for engaging in political recruitment and action in the slums. That is one of the most meaningful forms of work in this society. And there should be a guaranteed annual income so that a man—if he has not already been twisted out of the possibility of self-recognition in school —can *work* at finding and fulfilling his potential instead of at dreary routines that machines are so well equipped to do so much more efficiently.

At this point, of course, I am being what the bland, well-meaning middle class—characterized to me by the editorial writers of the *New York Times*—would call "utopian." And, alas, it is not enough to answer them with Bayard Rustin's utterly correct observation: "These are times when that which is not utopian is not relevant." Most of those in the larger society haven't the slightest idea of what Rustin means. As R. H. S. Crossman once pointed out, ". . . if you create an affluent majority, it will prove even more selfish and hard-hearted than the wealthy minority which it replaces." And those middle-class values which are paramount in this society today are selfishness, hypocrisy, and a deep, bitter resentment against being disturbed—against having to *read* about riots in the ghetto, against having to *see* riots on television.

I do agree that as cybernation swallows up more of the once affluent majority, some of the suddenly empoored or those made suddenly obsolete will gain empathy with the underclass. And it may well be that we will not have the kind of political coalition which can change the way the underclass lives until the underclass and its allies among the "left-outs" are in the majority—if by then basic change is still possible. What I am saying about the present, however, is that until and unless the youngsters we are trying to motivate get a real sense that they are not still being lied to, we are not going to begin to remove their sense of alienation.

They will have to see basic changes in their schools—in teachers and curricula and in the end of that track system. They will have to be trained in work skills by those who are not patronizing them or regarding them as animals at bay and who have an awareness that there are qualities in the slum life style which the middle class could well emulate. I am not ro-manticizing here, and would refer you to the work of Frank Riessman and Edgar Friedenberg, among others, for elabora-tion. And preferably, throughout any of these skirmishes against poverty, many more of what the social workers call "indigenous personnel" should be involved in training and otherwise dealing with the "disadvantaged" young. I mean a greatly intensified enlistment of people from the ghetto who either have the requisite abilities to teach and administer or who have those capacities and can learn. And just as basically, if we are going to train a youngster in a specific work skill in one of these programs, we ought to have a real job waiting for him when he finishes and there ought to be reserves of money to assure him that he can keep going back for more retraining as his careers change because of galloping cybernation. Putting it another way, the degree and depth of planning that can make these fledgling "War on Poverty" projects mean anything at all—except as political rhetoric—is not yet in evidence.

But fundamentally—and this is at the base of everything I've tried to say in this paper—nothing will work in the long run for the masses of the poor until we have the kind of political re- alignment in this country which will produce Congressmen who will vote for the expenditures and the planning necessary to eradicate poverty. (We already have the resources.) Only then can we really begin to redefine work. And if we ever get to that point—and to the kind of educational system consonant with that kind of society—there should be no major problems in motivating youth to stay in school and to make a commit- ment to the larger society. Because then that larger society will not be the society we know now.

We are a long way from the kind of society that, paradoxi- cally, is well within our capacity to create. And I am not sanguine that we will ever get there. If so mild an example of getting to the nitty-gritty of motivating the young as Mobiliza- tion for Youth has been emasculated, is there any realistic hope of knowledgeable support from Federal, state, and local government—or the foundations—for getting that underclass into a war on poverty *by* the poor? I doubt it. The poor, includ- ing the young among them, are still being lied to. The majority in this society—and they include far too many of the experts on delinquency and deprivation and motivation—do not want the way *they* themselves live to be basically changed. But until the way *everyone* lives—and the values by which he lives—is changed, all of these attacks on problems of delinquency and motivation are going to be fragmentary, and more involved with surface than substance.

The only answer I see is for that underclass—and whatever allies it can muster—to get political power so that at a future symposium such as this they will have most of the seats on the panel. The middle-class social scientist, let alone the middle-class foundation official or government official, however well-intentioned, is not radical enough to deal existentially with the problems of this symposium. There are, to be sure, exceptions, and a number of them are here. But they don't have the power and the access to the amounts of money that are needed. The "left-outs," therefore, must now build their own base of power, because the government—as it is now—is not going to finance a social revolution for them.

THE EXILES: DROPOUTS IN
THE AFFLUENT SOCIETY

by S. M. Miller

S. M. Miller, Professor of Education and Sociology at New York
University, is an advisor to the Ford Foundation and to the President's Committee on Juvenile Delinquency. Under grants from the
Ford Foundation and the National Science Foundation, he is engaged in research in social welfare policies and poverty, and social
mobility and economic change. His most recent book, coauthored
with Frank Riessman, is titled *Social Class and Social Policy*.

LOW-INCOME youths are under attack. They are portrayed as "unmotivated" toward school and work; characterized as "hard-to-reach" by those who feel a professional responsibility to provide social services to them; charged with an
unwillingness to take advantage of the various opportunities—
scholastic, occupational, and consultative—which are thrust
upon them. Indeed, some have concluded that we are in the
midst of an existential crisis of alienated youth repudiating the
glittering offerings of society.

At a more specific (and less glamorous) level, our low-
income youths are reported as rejecting the opportunities for
training and retraining that are now available to them. They
are problem children for they are unwilling ("unmotivated" is
the preferred term) to go through a training program which
will open up the doors to occupational success.

I fear that before we can charge low-income youth with unwillingness to seize opportunity, we must be certain that we
are presenting genuine hope.

We are developing a great many work-training programs for dropouts. As we increasingly find it difficult to deliver jobs, we emphasize training in "work motivation" rather than specific marketable work skills.[1] On one project, youths complained because they were shoveling manure.[2] What demon tricked them into believing that this experience was not increasing their employability?

The prospective rapid increase in work-training programs under the Economic Opportunity Act can be dangerous if there are insufficient jobs for those who have raked and motivated their ways through the training period. Not to deliver at the end of a training period is going to encourage apathy, withdrawal, and anger. Many low-income youths will be fooled again by professional Pied Pipers whose offer of hope is a hoax.

In the absence of real jobs for graduates, the danger is that these programs degenerate into mechanisms of social control under the guise of opportunity. In this respect I find that many observers share my growing anxiety about the use of group therapy-like sessions within training programs. At least some of these activities are highly manipulative, utilizing peer-group influences to change youth into a malleable form without affecting the forces impinging upon the environment they are in or the future that they face.

We must have, immediately, much more emphasis on insuring employment for youth. Training without a delivery is training for injustice. If we do get hundreds of thousands of youths into jobs, then the youth employment crisis ahead will be much

[1] Judith G. Benjamin, *Programs to Make Youth Employable*. New York, National Committee on Employment of Youth, 1964. This is a summary of *Youth Employment Programs in Perspective*, a report of the Youth-Work Program Review of the National Committee on Employment of Youth.
[2] S. M. Miller and Ira Harrison, "Types of Dropouts—'The Unemployables,'"

graver than the one we now face. It is one thing to persuade the unemployed to get training; another to tell those trained that they have been fooled.

SELECTIVE STIMULATION

The private economy is unlikely to deliver the jobs under present conditions. Its expansion is not great enough to provide many new jobs, and the nature of the labor demand is not for low-skill personnel. We need to make a concerted effort to increase jobs at the low-skill levels (without taking jobs away from more skilled individuals).

Industries employing low-skill personnel in large numbers have to be encouraged to expand. This might be done through rebates on unemployment insurance payments or through lower corporation tax rates for firms which have a low ratio of net profits to the nonmanagerial wage bill. Selective mechanisms rather than the aggregate, across-the-board instruments of now-traditional Keynesian policy are necessary to increase employment in *particular* sectors of industry.

I think that we have to overcome the liberal prejudice that only the expansion of Federal activities can be of social benefit. We need to think of ways to induce the private sector to do socially useful things. I don't altogether like this, but I don't see a viable alternative today.

This is not to argue against the needed increase in the absolute size of the public sector, if not its size relative to the gross national product. Here again, we have to focus on selective measures if we wish to assure employment for youths and other low-skilled individuals.

Secretary of Labor Willard Wirtz has lamented that the

in Arthur Shostak and William Gomberg, eds., *Blue-Collar World* (Englewood Cliffs, N.J., Prentice-Hall, 1964).

United States lacks a major new job-creating industry. An additional industry providing 3 to 5 million additional jobs could soak up present-day unemployment. But *any* kind of industry would not do this. What are needed are enterprises and agencies requiring the kind of labor that could be provided by unemployed low-income youths and adults. One suggestion, which Arthur Pearl and Frank Riessman among others have urged, is the development of nonprofessional or subprofessional roles in the social services.[3] These new positions would permit the needed expansion of social services despite the prevailing shortage of professionally trained personnel. They would also lead to a new quality and to new kinds of service by utilizing persons as service-dispensers who are similar in background to the recipients of service.

Another suggestion, proffered by Richard Boone, is to encourage the development of specific youth industries. One such activity would be to subsidize restaurants, dance halls, cafes, and radio and television stations, specifically oriented to and run by youth. Youth's interest in consumption and entertainment would be tied to expanding employment opportunities for youth.

One of the problems with the expansion of employment for youth is that most of the new occupations would be dead ends, not leading to higher levels of occupational competence and employment potential. Training of various kinds must be *continuously available* so that it is possible to move up or to shift from one type of activity to another.

Hopefully, having some positive employment experience and being older may improve the chances of getting jobs in the regular labor market. But some mechanisms of transfer from specialized employment markets (like the subprofessional) to the

---

[3] Arthur Pearl and Frank Riessman, *New Careers for the Poor: The Nonprofessional in Human Services* (New York, The Free Press, 1965).

regular labor market is probably necessary. If not, the special markets for youth or unskilled labor will have to grow enormously as millions of new workers look for jobs and those already in the specialized markets stay in them because no other opportunities exist.

Obviously, some labor market policy is necessary. What happens to youth will affect what happens to adults and to youths when they become adults. If there really are three million jobs not being filled, then can we not induce skilled employed workers to become further skilled to fill these jobs and leave their present jobs? These jobs in turn could become available to others moving up, creating opportunities down the line. Vested pension rights, adequate rather than minimum subsistence levels for training and moving allowances would be necessary.

Inducements to open plants in particular areas or to have a particular mix of employees (like the requirement in some nations that a set proportion of the employees be physically handicapped persons) could be extended. Special, temporary programs could provide employment for those not taken care of through the usual labor market channels. Graded employment experience could funnel into higher-level jobs, so that age would be accompanied by more pay and responsibility.

The Federal government in conjunction with state and local governments, private enterprise, and nonprofit agencies could flexibly move toward implementing the goal of full employment for youth. Inducements to private enterprise, regular governmentally supported employment activities, and special programs for particular needs and period, all are needed.

EDUCATION AND TRAINING

A central element—second only to government activity in stimulating or providing new jobs—is the expansion and improvement of education and training. Here, it seems to be clear that more is not enough. We need better, more appropriate, more effective education and training.

We have to develop a policy for job-training in the schools. I avoid the term vocational education because that has tended to have a more specific meaning. We are at a loss for answers to some fundamental questions. What is the appropriate role for schools in the job field? How specifically should youth be prepared for local jobs? How carefully should training be tied in with local industry? What proportion of time should be spent in the job-training program? How intimately should the regular school program be tied in with job-training in the schools? These are value questions, not technical questions.

I would support a strong job inlay in schools if we recognize the school and training programs as flexible, adaptable instruments providing many points of entry and reentry into the educational system. We have to get away from the notion that everyone should go through public school in twelve continuous years and college in four. Individuals drop out of the educational apparatus and are helped—sometimes actively encouraged and financed—to reenter it. A withdrawal from school should not be a permanent state. Entering a particular vocational program does not preclude later transfer into college-preparation programs. This is not easy to do in practice.

The school has to be restructured so that more students can stay to graduate and become equipped for college. Those who want to reenter at any point should be able to do so, even if it means that they must be financed in their second, third, or fourth tries. At present, little special effort is made to bring back dropout youths, with the exception of summer campaigns (or attacks) to persuade them to return. But no effort is expended to change the school so that reentry is a *live second chance* rather than an admission of failure or mistake. We have to recognize that training and retraining are going to be continuously taking place in the lifetime of workers. Our institutions of education and training must accept this as a social fact which is basic to their planning and organization. Administrative flexibility (as well as sizable funds) is central to the ability to deal with problems of adapting skills to changing technology. A lot more money will have to be spent on education. Today, 70 percent more is spent annually on new cars than on all public education.

It would be helpful to have individuals in the neighborhoods serving as links between the school and the dropouts, helping the latter to make contact with the schools, facilitating adjustment to school. In a sense, they could be community counselors helping people thread their way through educational and social services. The counselor could be one of the new subprofessional roles.

I would like to see storefront colleges and college divisions in low-income neighborhoods. The closer a school and neighborhood is to a college, the more likely are the youths to go on to college. We should rule out the financial factor in attending colleges, providing not only free tuition but also subsistence payments to all students who need it. The Economic Opportunity Act permits this. The funds should be expended so that they induce those who would not have been able to think of going to college, to now begin it. Students of low-income schools should be guaranteed jobs so that they can go on to college.

Vocational education as presently conducted is scandalous. We have to learn more about the occupational future, decide on what kinds of occupations to train youth for, and learn how to teach the needed skills. I am sadly impressed after repair work on my car or household appliances that we do not know how to teach many skills.

Vocational education is in the throes of a value choice between elite, technical education for high-level students and "vocational" education which serves as a warehouse for low-level students. I think the former will get the school attention and the rejects from the elite programs will be encouraged to drift out of school into the new work-training programs.

This would be disturbing. Vocational education, which had not been much concerned with the problems of pedagogy, has to learn to improve its performance with school-problem youth. This is one of the great challenges of vocational education which should not be avoided by the emphasis on technical education.

One useful strategy is to prepare retraining programs for present (and future) teachers of vocational subjects. These could be summer programs like those for mathematics or language teachers, and could emphasize not only content but the severely neglected problems of teaching "low-motivated" youth.

YOUTHFUL DIVERSITY

The diversity among low-income, dropout youth is insufficiently recognized. Some dropouts are of high intellectual quality with great potential. They should be encouraged to move on to college. Others could improve their employment potential somewhat by staying on to high-school graduation. Like the potential college group, they may need temporary training or other aid to help move them into school. Others who have limited academic prowess can do well in jobs; their problem is effective placement on jobs in which they can be trained and upgraded. Still others are difficult to place and to keep on a job. They need experience but can develop fairly rapidly. Finally, there is an extremely difficult group of dropouts—perhaps 20 percent—who need considerably longer-term help.

Unfortunately, we do not have varied programs to deal with these varied youths. Because of the inability to deliver jobs, we are increasingly emphasizing training in "work motivation" rather than in specific skills. While this *may* be appropriate for the last two groups (the marginal and the problem youth), it is doubtful if it is for the first three (the high-education potential, the stable working class, and the placement-needy). Indeed, one frequently gets the impression that some of the problem group are thought to need some form of psychological treatment and that the work group is regarded as a therapeutic environment and experience. Sometimes this is true, but considering the way many of these programs are run, one cannot be sanguine about the therapeutic value of fresh air or leaf-raking—the modern-day equivalents of basket-weaving for the mentally retarded or disturbed.

Our training programs have to be oriented to the great variations among our unemployed or underemployed (in terms of job level) youths. We are in some ways stereotyping the dropouts into glamorous "alienateds," when the problem is that we do not have jobs for many who do want to work.

There is no magic solution. It will take money to provide more jobs and better training for youth. We cannot phony this. If we make even an implicit commitment to provide employment after training, we have to deliver. There has to be an *authenticity* about our concern about youth. We do not want just to lower the juvenile delinquency rate but to see that more youth have a crack at enjoying life. In the absence of this authentic concern about youth, most of our programs will be finger exercises for the professional trainers and requiems for hopeful youth.

To be poor in America is to be an exile in one's own country. To demand responsibility of youth without providing positions for them in society is adult self-deception. Commitment, imagination, and education are needed to reduce the worsening crisis of youth unemployment. Old institutions must be reshaped, revitalized and adequately financed. New institutions must be formed. But they cannot be façades to hide reality.

THE ROLE OF TRAINING IN MEETING THE NEEDS OF UNEMPLOYED YOUTH

by Marcia K. Freedman

Marcia K. Freedman, a research social scientist in the Conservation of Human Resources Project at Columbia University, was Director of the Youth-Work Program Review of the National Committee on Employment of Youth from 1963 to 1965. She is the author of numerous articles and studies, and is an advisor to the President's Committee on Juvenile Delinquency and Youth Crime and the President's Committee on Law Enforcement and Administration of Justice.

TRAINING implies the creation of competence. In more primitive times it was learned through graded participation in adult concerns. Even now, much that is utilized in actual job performance is picked up informally, by trial and error, by "hanging around." But as production and service functions become more complex, and as more people complete more years of schooling, requirements for occupational mobility go up. No longer can a messenger boy rise by degrees to middle management. Recruits for such status are drawn from the ranks of the holders of graduate degrees and broken in (or discarded) through elaborate patterns of training. The higher the job level, the lengthier and more complex is the training; and the higher the requirements, the more likely is the preemployment phase of training to be institutionalized.

In fact, the identification of higher education with vocational preparation has elicited cries of despair from those who see the civilizing values of education undermined by vulgar preoccupation with the "better job." The other side of the picture—where less skilled jobs are concerned—exhibits the following features: low turnover among males in stable organizations; higher educational requirements; growing rigidity of occupational classification with less room for upward mobility; and rising age of entry into the labor force. Those looking for work with evidence that they have completed a course of pre-employment training are very likely to find a job, *if* their field is one in which such training is acceptable to employers. Where training is at the secondary-school level, the assumption that students can successfully be prepared for immediate employment works out best in fields dominated by young women —clerical, retailing, and practical nursing. Girl high school graduates in these fields readily find jobs, but young men who have completed a secondary school vocational course are not always so fortunate. In the better organized, more highly skilled trades, their high school training does not obviate the need to complete an apprenticeship, but neither does it serve as an entering wedge. In service occupations, general disorganization both in training and recruiting makes the present uncertain and the future hazardous.

Although all studies agree that blue-collar workers have in the main learned their skills informally, the fact is that opportunities to learn by doing on the job are more and more constricted. Employers, many of whom are themselves unwilling or unable to furnish such informal training opportunities, are still looking for workers with experience gained "elsewhere." Attempts to legitimate secondary school preemployment training have had sporadic success, usually when groups of employers have made specific the conditions upon which the preemployment training will be recognized.

Over all, however, the variety of opinion in most communities on the usefulness of secondary school occupational preparation has the effect of a gigantic fugue, marked not by the mathematical certainties of Bach, but by the most clashing dissonance. For the youths who are caught up in this furor, the general rule is that those whose preparation is judged to be inadequate are most likely to have trouble finding a job in the first place, and are least likely to have access to further training once they are employed.[1]

It is these youths who are the subject of the Symposium. Their unemployment rate has remained disturbingly high even during the current boom. Just as significant is their marginal attachment to the labor force. In a study of 100 metropolitan areas, Bowen and Finegan found that both in 1950 and in 1960, the labor force participation rate of teenage males responded to changes in the local unemployment rate more than any other group.[2] Those at the margins are established neither in an occupation nor in a job, and their sporadic work experiences are of little help in their vocational development.

In the most general terms, there are two public policy approaches for dealing with such symptoms of malfunction. One is to manipulate or change certain features of the structure; the other is to manipulate or change individuals who do not fit into the structure. In recent years we have had both, but the former has been limited almost entirely to fiscal manipulations such as the tax cut, which taken alone have fallen short with respect to demand for labor. Meanwhile, programs at all levels of government and through private initiative have concentrated on attempts to change individuals. Particularly since 1962, train-

[1] National Committee on Employment of Youth. *Getting Hired, Getting Trained* (Washington, Government Printing Office, 1965).
[2] William G. Bowen and T. A. Finegan, "Labor Force Participation and Unemployment," in Arthur M. Ross, ed., *Employment Policy and the Labor Market* (Berkeley, University of California Press, 1965).

ing has become an important ingredient in the "rehabilitation" of the unemployed. It is the purpose of this paper to explore some of the issues related to this policy emphasis.

Training has come into the forefront for youth, first as an additional element when earlier efforts have proved insufficient, and second as an outgrowth of theoretical notions on the nature of unemployment. Because we have not had a repetition of the catastrophic unemployment of the thirties, there are those who conclude that our current problem is limited largely to the mismatch of workers and available jobs. The major evidence adduced is the existence of unfilled jobs in some communities alongside relatively high unemployment rates. But this tends to be a frictional situation in the same sense that a 2 percent unemployment rate is considered frictional. At unemployment rates above 3 percent, vacancies exist for a time and are then filled; there is nothing permanent about them. Furthermore, they reflect a lag in opportunities for higher education, since most of them require the kind of acceptable, high-level preemployment training described above.

If, indeed, existing vacancies represented a serious manpower shortage, the solution would be to upgrade presently underemployed workers, thus making room at the bottom, particularly for unskilled young entry workers. The MDTA of 1962 makes such provision, but the number of people involved in on-the-job training for this purpose has been only a fraction of the total MDTA effort. Quite apart from special legislation, there is not even much evidence that companies offering tuition refund benefits to their employees have used their own resources in any organized way to achieve this result. In fact, a good deal of company emphasis in training has always been on improving performance rather than on upgrading.

In general terms, those who are charged with the establishment of training programs for youth have had to choose, from the 30,000-odd occupations in the *Dictionary of Occupational Titles*, those kinds of work which require a relatively brief training period and on which there is agreement on appropriate preemployment training. The training furthermore must be within the immediate grasp of the desired target group; and there must be reasonable expectation of employment upon completion of the program. These, roughly, were the original criteria established for MDTA. Their restrictiveness made it difficult to serve the hard-core unemployed, and particularly young men.

Even before the 1963 amendments to the Act, concern for this failure led to an administrative change that reserved available funds for the nineteen-to-twenty-one age group for special projects "designed to meet the needs of underprivileged youth in areas where youth employment is a serious problem." In effect, this order resulted in a shift of emphasis subsequently embodied in the amendments. Instead of first selecting an occupation and then recruiting trainees, it became possible to recruit unemployed youth and to establish a program for them. The amendments had the further effect of making the seventeen- and eighteen-year-olds eligible for training allowances, provided they were out of school for at least one year, and expanding the proportion of training allowances for youth to 25 percent of the total number of allowances paid. The amendments also broadened the concept of training to cover "basic educational skills"—in effect, literacy training—in combination with occupational training, and added twenty weeks to the original limit of fifty-two weeks for this purpose.

Perhaps the biggest change in direction signified by the MDTA amendments—a change which has also occurred in other areas of youth employment programing—is the introduction of the concept of "employability." Early requirements of "a reasonable expectation of employment" were the greatest stumbling block in the establishment of training, particularly since local administrators always tended to interpret it very narrowly. In some depressed communities of Pennsylvania, for example, State efforts to establish retraining programs several years before the enactment of MDTA were severely hampered by such interpretations. The shift to "employability" changed program emphasis from the creation of skill to the goal of individual rehabilitation.

Logically, this shift should have the effect of making programing more flexible, but the difficulty here is that flexibility is only of use in a graded series of programs. In the absence of a full range of programing, "employability" can readily become a regressive rather than a progressive concept. This is particularly clear in the youth field. Among unemployed young people, there undoubtedly exists a group (the size of which is not easily ascertainable) who are unemployable under *any* labor market conditions. These are youths who out of either hostility or ignorance have developed a kind of antiwork ethic. Some of them are second- or third-generation welfare dependents, some have been recently released from training institutions for delinquents, and some are simply bewildered by their total ignorance of what goes on outside the parochial confines of their own neighborhood. For such youths, and particularly those under eighteen, a rehabilitative effort is clearly required before any kind of occupational training can begin. But this type of rehabilitation is not training in the sense of the creation of occupational competence; it focuses, rather, on conditioning to the idea of work.

However, all unemployed youth who need help do not fit into the group just described. Particularly after they reach eighteen, many tend to settle down and accept the discipline of work. There may be some who need elaborate remediation, but there are others who simply need jobs. Furthermore, all those brands saved from the burning—those who have successfully passed through a conditioning phase—must then go on either to training, employment, or both. When all is said and done, expectation of employment *is* the key issue. Young trainees can be motivated to adequate performance by the existence of a job; and in the long run, all the rehabilitation in the world is of no value without a place to use it. Where programs begin and end at the conditioning level, they would seem to be of scant benefit. If they are to be meaningful, they must afford further developmental opportunity.

It is at this point that programing tends to break down, since the next step depends on the existence either of jobs or of career lines for which training can be organized. In fact, the relative success of programs may often be traced to variations in local labor market conditions. This effect is so great that there is a temptation to question the need for special youth-training programs. They tend to be introduced as a solution for the employment problems of youth, when in fact they work best in the presence of real labor shortages.

For any particular group of youths, one way around this paradox is to combine the training opportunity with some aid in negotiating the system. The most promising examples of this approach have been the "coupled" programs which have combined institutional and on-the-job training for mutual support. This was the case in the National Institute for Labor Education Youth Employment Program (NILE-YEP), which developed agreements with unions and employers for Training for Apprenticeship (TFA). TFA provided a preliminary training period in conjunction with a standard apprenticeship program.

The simple logic of the TFA is this: Since it was the objective of the NILE-YEP to open up skilled training opportunities for school dropouts, and since it would have been unwise and obviously fruitless to persuade unions and management to lower standards of entrance and training, established over a long period of time, it followed that efforts had to be made to up-grade the knowledge and skill of school dropouts so that they would at least appoximate the standards required of applicants for an apprenticeship in a given trade or industry. This, it was concluded, could be accomplished by requiring disadvantaged youth to take training of varying length, both on-the-job and institutional, as a prerequisite for acceptance into the apprenticeship system. . . .

The *TFA concept* provides an unusual opportunity and powerful incentive for youngsters who are unable to meet the required standards, to enter a skilled trade under sheltered conditions. Although the youngster has to accept an additional training period —over and above his regular apprenticeship—he is being paid while overcoming the deficiencies of his education and he is also assured of transfer into the regular apprenticeship after satisfactory completion of the TFA, and with it, of eventually becoming a skilled craftsman.[3]

In two years NILE negotiated successfully for some 600 youths. Quite apart from the question of trainee success or access to job openings, the report of the project documents the enormous institutional hazards to such a program effort, including not only the resistance of union and management, but also the competing demands and regulations of Federal agencies and their state and local counterparts. NILE, in effect, ran interference for those who otherwise could never have entered apprenticeship.

[3] Joan Bowers, "Skill Obsolescence and Re-Education," *White House Conference on Education*. U.S. Senate, Subcommittee on Education of the Committee on Labor and Public Welfare. 89th Cong., 1st Sess. (Washington, Government Printing Office, 1965, pp. 24–34). See also National Institute of Labor Education, Youth Employment Program, "Final Report to the Secretary of Labor, United States Department of Labor, on OMAT Project P 3–63" (Washington, The Institute, 1965).

Such aid in negotiating the system seems also to be a part of the planning of the Job Corps. Participation in the program results in the acquisition of new types of credentials which substitute for more traditional diplomas, quite apart from the degree of skill acquired. And employers are urged to hire those who have completed training, as part of a national effort. Whereas the NILE program resulted in starting some youths on the path to craftsmanship, the Job Corps' effort is far less clear with respect to training goals.

The issue of job creation has been approached gingerly, if at all, in the new programs established by the Economic Opportunity Act. For example, the conservation activities in which about one-half of the Job Corps enrollees are engaged are not attached to a plan for expansion of conservation with the concomitant creation of a large number of permanent new jobs. The experiences of young men in the "rural" camps might lead them to careers in conservation, but only if long-range plans are made for employment and training.

A somewhat similar problem arises in the Neighborhood Youth Corps Programs. The stated purpose is "to provide useful work experience opportunities for unemployed young men and young women, through participation in state and community work-training programs, so that their employability may be increased or their education resumed and continued and so that public agencies and private nonprofit organizations (other than political parties) will be enabled to carry out programs which will permit or contribute to an undertaking or service in the public interest that would otherwise not be provided, or will contribute to the conservation and development of natural resources and recreational areas." [4]

Here again, no permanent increase in public service is con-

[4] U.S. Congress. *Economic Opportunity Act of 1964*, Title 1B. 88th Cong., 2nd Sess.

templated. One concrete example is in the further requirement of the Act that programs "will not result in the displacement of employed workers under existing contract or services." The urban renewal needs of the United States have been estimated at figures up to $1 trillion. Ninety percent of the assets involved are privately owned, but even the 10 percent in the public sector represent enormous opportunities to employ people in useful tasks. Designated conservation and urban renewal areas in the big cities could utilize the manpower of a great many youths in such varied activities as relocation and home-making assistance, repair and renovation (outside of plumbing, heating, and wiring), the creation and maintenance of recreation areas, and a host of similar services.

But unions in the construction trades may have very real objections to such employment of youngsters in a period characterized by large swings in the demand for building-trade workers. The solution to this problem would seem again to lie in planning for the long range. For example, if the nation as a whole agreed on a given level of investment in renewal activities over a relatively long period of time, the resistance of unions might well collapse in the face of guaranteed employment of their members. Journeymen could, among other activities, act as supervisors for young workers who might subsequently be taken into vastly expanded apprenticeship or modified training programs of the type negotiated through NILE.

In the implementation of the Act as it stands, the largest users of available youth will probably be municipalities. The rise in government employment in the last decade has been largely at the state and local level, and all cities anticipate the need for more personnel and services. Enrolling youths on a pre–civil-service level may actually provide city governments with a cadre of better trained personnel (particularly for low-level jobs) than they had before. But again, the implicit promise must be made explicit. One model is now in operation in New York City under the Municipal Coop Program. There, city government has joined the ranks of employers who hire high school students part time as a training device, with the assumption that a significant proportion will go on to regular civil service employment.

The Act requires that trainees perform useful work as well as receive training. These two criteria have created problems in the past, as far back as the National Youth Administration.[5] Generally, one mandate is carried out to the detriment of the other. The supervisor of a work-training group in a municipal park, for example, may well be tempted to make a good impression by having his charges concentrate on the least skilled cleanup tasks, while investing relatively little in the imparting of new skills. The danger here is that the program will regress to a mere device for keeping young people off the regular labor market, and at worst to that species of leaf-raking so much deplored by opponents of public works. The work involved, in order to be truly useful, must bring benefits to the trainees. In the long run, they are the resources that are most important to conserve, but this goal requires a high level of supervisory patience and, perhaps just as important, the promise of a more adult form of employment as the candidate proves himself worthy.

The new national programs can provide us with an opportunity to make certain assessments—about needed activities in conservation, possibilities of rationalizing training, the potential of presently disenfranchised youth, and the need for at-

[5] L. L. Lorwin, *Youth Work Programs: Problems and Policies* (Washington, American Council on Education, 1941).

tacking problems at a more basic level than we have heretofore been willing to do. If these things can be accomplished, the money expended under the poverty legislation and under such programs as MDTA will bring an important return.

If, on the other hand, the public expects permanent solutions for the problems of youth employment out of this legislation, one can confidently predict their disappointment. Faced with the uncertainties of the general level of employment and the nature of the occupational structure, our guideposts for rehabilitation are few and far between. Training, like counseling and other elements of program, should not be elevated to a policy. It is intrinsically important, but by itself it cannot cope with all the problems youth now faces in making an orderly transition from school to work, from dependence to maturity.[6]

[6] See R. S. Eckaus, "Economic Criteria for Education and Training," *Review of Economics and Statistics*, 36 (May 1964), pp. 181–90; and Sar A. Levitan, *Federal Manpower Policies and Programs to Combat Unemployment* (Kalamazoo, Michigan, The W. E. Upjohn Institute for Employment Research, 1964).

PLANNING FOR LEISURE

by W. H. Ferry

W. H. Ferry is Vice President of the Center for the Study of Democratic Institutions and a frequent contributor to the Center's publications. He was a partner of Earl Newsom and Company, a New
York public relations firm, for nine years, and has worked in various educational, editorial, public relations, and advisory capacities. His newspaper work included reporting in this country and
in South America. This article was excerpted from *Caught in the
Horn of Plenty,* published by the Center for the Study of Democratic Institutions, Santa Barbara, California.

THE UNITED STATES, as everyone knows, has grown
less and less capitalistic over many years. Capitalism relates
work and reward, investment and jobs, scarcity and incentives.
Automation, the principal progenitor of technological unemployment, is adding heavy qualifications to all of these propositions. Automation and its technological cousins may prove to
be the main destroyers of what is left of capitalism, just as
technology has been the destroyer of the theory of small-scale,
family farm agriculture.

The discussion of what a development like automation
means is crippled by archaic terms of reference. Economic
phenomena today are considered in the framework and with
the glossary of classical analysis. Even the least sophisticated
observer knows that the determining forces in the economy today are not the same as they were in Adam Smith's time, or as
they were even in the nineteenth century. Science and technology are accomplishing as thorough a revolution in social and
economic theory as they are in the theory of war and interna-

tional relations. Allocation of resources is today a secondary question; the primary question is just distribution, for which we have no economic theory or technique.

Our growing inability to absorb available workers into the economy will give this question of "just" distribution a point it has never before had. These technologically displaced people will comprise a new class, which I shall hereafter refer to as the "liberated margin." The members of this group will be freed—permanently liberated—from traditional toil, not because they want it so, but because the imperatives of efficiency have sent them to the sidelines. The liberated margin is as challenging a subject for social theorists as exists in our day. The members of this group personify abundance. No economic theory provides for a liberated margin. We have no guide to thinking about such a class of citizens. Many questions arise. How will they live? Who will provide for them? What should be the community's attitude?

The immemorial view is that unemployment is a bad state of affairs. Although all the tendencies in recent generations have been toward leisure—shorter workdays and workweeks, more pay for less labor, education for constructive use of spare time —the country has assumed that the process would always come to a convenient halt close to the Full Employment sign. It seems not to have occurred to any statesman that leisure might as readily be a goal of society as employment. Now that such a possibility exists, no welcome mat is put out for it. On the contrary, dismay is the rule. Instead of embracing the hope that technology may be opening the way into a new style of civilization, one in which work and the economic machinery are not the preeminent concerns of society, the effort today is to show that nothing has been significantly altered by the onrush of technology, that we can lean back comfortably on ancient theories, and that old goals are best after all.

This attitude is particularly evident in the discussion of structural unemployment. For generations the dictum that Machines Make Jobs was demonstrably valid. Now the dictum is losing its force and generality. Machines are replacing workers. Some part of the 50,000 new jobs that have to be provided weekly to keep the American economy going are, to be sure, being supplied by new machines. But what the machine giveth at one place it taketh away at another: hence, structural unemployment.

The question is whether jobs can be manufactured fast enough to approach full employment, using the present definition of jobs and the means of providing them that are presently regarded as acceptable. The essential contention of this paper is that the answer is "No." An apparently unavoidable condition of the Age of Abundance is increasing structural unemployment and underemployment.

The novelty of this proposition is that the majority of victims of technological displacement will be *permanently* out of work. They will not just be "resting between engagements." They will not just be waiting for the next upturn, or for expansion of the industry or company in which they were working. They will no longer be the objects of unemployment insurance plans, for these plans are designed to fill the gap between jobs, not to provide a permanent dole.

The center of the difficulty is the rapidly emerging fact that every year from now on we shall be able, because of accelerating technology, to produce the goods and services needed by the nation with fewer and fewer of the available hands—say 90 percent or less.

I use the phrase "90 percent or less" advisedly. It is a delicate way of bringing in the touchy issues of featherbedding and underemployment. Everyone knows what featherbedding means. Underemployment describes workers who continue to hold jobs after it has been established that machines can do the jobs as well or better, or people who work only part time. The underemployed, according to some authorities, total as high as 25 percent of the labor force. The underemployed include also a million or more agricultural workers who stay on the farm because there is no work in industry for them, 5,000,000 women who would like jobs, and 2,000,000 part-time workers. Note must be taken also of double jobholding—moonlighting —by hundreds of thousands of workers.

The unemployed and underemployed are no longer almost exclusively the unskilled, the recent immigrants, the colored, the groups at the end of the economic scale, who have customarily borne the heaviest weight of economic slides. White-collar workers are joining this group as automation reaches the office. There is some reason for thinking that in a few years white-collar workers will comprise most of the growing category of technologically displaced.

Harvey Swados remarked some time ago in a brilliant essay that the question of work would be the biggest domestic political issue of the 1960s. Part of his argument was that accelerating technological displacement would harden into an established economic pattern; the country would sooner or later be driven to the knowledge that it is not dealing with a regrettable but transient phenomenon. And, Swados said, there is a serious question whether Americans can accommodate themselves either to the idea or to the use of abundant leisure. The revolutionary consequences of leisure in a nation committed to economic dynamism and to work, any kind of work, as a good in itself have found no radical echoes yet in public policy.

Mention of the word planning rouses instant suspicion. When coupled with the word national—that is, national planning—it sends editorial writers headlong to their typewriters. Yet national planning is indispensable if the United States is going to make sense out of its future. Can anyone imagine an unplanned transition from war to peace production, or an unplanned highway program? For those willing to acknowledge that free enterprise is not a divine dispensation and capitalism not a dictate of natural law, the need is evident everywhere.

The essential elements of the program proposed here are: First, national planning authorized by Congress, and not national planning administered by a bureaucratic ogre to be appointed by the CIO, the NAM, or the ADA. Second, a scheme based on what W. Arthur Lewis calls "planning by inducement,"[1] by which he means the use of politics and persuasion, in their various guises, to achieve a more reasonable utilization of resources and a better distribution of income. Finally, recognition of today's economic order for what it is, an enormously complicated piece of machinery which cannot be run by the instruction manuals of the eighteenth and nineteenth centuries. In few places does national hypocrisy have as many facets as in the simplistic rhetoric of the opponents of planning. The most violent antiplanners are the same men who expertly plan the future of their corporations for ten to thirty years, and who rely on planners to keep their suburbs from infestation by junkyards and filling stations.

National planning will be recognition that the government bears the final responsibility for the quality and content and prosperity of the nation. This may perhaps be called modern mercantilism. Those who construe these proposals as some dark version of new and unholy economic doctrines are advised to refer to economic planning in sixteenth and seventeenth cen-

[1] *The Principles of Economic Planning* (London, Dobson, 1958), Chapter One.

tury England or, even better, to the economic history of the Eastern seaboard of this country in the eighteenth and early nineteenth centuries.

In an abundant society the problem is not an economic one of keeping the machine running regardless of what they put out, but a political one of achieving the common good. And planning is one of the major means of attaining the common good.

But whether or not we can figure out some such way of taking systematic advantage of the bewildering fact of abundance, we shall within a short while have to discard attitudes that grew up in the dog-eat-dog phase of capitalism and adopt others suitable to modern mercantilism. For example, we shall have to stop automatically regarding the unemployed as lazy, unlucky, indolent, and unworthy. We shall have to find means, public or private, of paying people to do no work.

This suggestion goes severely against the American grain, and it will have to be adopted slowly. The first steps have been taken. Unemployment insurance and supplementary unemployment benefit plans reached by management-union negotiations are examples. As these have come to be accepted as civic-industrial policy, so may plans for six-month work years, or retirement at fifty or fifty-five at full pay until pension schemes take hold. So may continuation of education well into adult years, at public expense. So may payment from the public treasury for nonproductive effort, such as writing novels, painting pictures, composing music, doing graduate work, and taking part in the expanding functions of government. Is a physicist more valuable to the community than a playwright? Why? The responsibility of the individual to the general welfare runs far beyond the purely economic.

The essential change in outlook will be to regard the new

leisure—including the leisure of the liberated margin—as desirable, as a good, and to direct public policy to accepting it as a good in itself.

This suggests some but far from all of the changes in conventional attitudes that will be compelled the moment that full employment is seen to be an obsolescent goal, and abandoned.

It will be hard to look on members of the liberated margin as useful participants in society, no matter how enlightened the arrangements may be, because "useful" has up to now strictly denoted people who work for economically productive enterprises and ends. Let me emphasize that I am not talking about idleness, only about what most people today regard as idleness, or near to it. The revolution in economic theory that is indicated by abundance is dramatically illustrated here. Whoever heard of economic theory with poets, painters, and philosophers among the premises?

Deliberation on the ways and the standards for getting purchasing power into the hands of the liberated margin may be the beginning of methodical social justice in the American political economy. Abundance may compel social justice as conscience never has. The liberated margin will have to get "what is its due." This means developing a basis of distribution of income which is not tied to work as a measure. For decisions about "due-ness" will have to be made without economic criteria; at least without the criterion of what members of the liberated margin are worth in the employment market, for there is no such market for them. The criteria of capitalism, are, in fact, largely irrelevant to conditions of abundance. Efficiency, administration, progress, success, profit, competition, and private gain are words of high standing in the lexicon of capitalism. Presumably among these terms are some of the "pseudo-moral principles" that Keynes saw on their way to the ashcan as society progressively solved its economic problems. In any event, a community of abundance will find less use for these ideas, and will turn instead to ideas like justice, law, government, general welfare, virtue, cooperation, and public responsibility as the touchstones of policy.

Abundance will enable a reversal of the old order of things. Modern mercantilism will remove the economic machine from the middle of the landscape to one side, where, under planning by inducement, its ever more efficient automata will provide the goods and services required by the general welfare. Humanity, with its politics and pastimes and poetry and conversation, will then occupy the central place in the landscape. Management of machines for human ends, not management by them, is the true object of industrial civilization.

This is the promise of modern mercantilism, and if the time is not yet, it is yet a time worth striving for. Meanwhile, the chief necessity is to revive respect for law and government as the proper instruments of the general welfare. Without this respect the economic future of this country and that of other nations linked to it will be determined, and stultified, by the accidents of private ambition and the hope of private gain. With this respect the Age of Abundance can be made into the Age of the General Welfare, and the United States can become in fact the moral commonwealth it has always claimed to be.

THE U.S. EMPLOYMENT SERVICE
IN PERSPECTIVE

by Edward T. Chase

Edward T. Chase, the author of numerous magazine articles, is
Editorial Vice President of New American Library. He has served,
in an advisory capacity, the U.S. Department of Commerce, the
Committee for Economic Development, the Henry Street Settlement, the Child Study Association, Group Health Insurance, Inc.,
the Urban League, *Flight Forum,* the Committee for Medical
Development, and Mobilization for Youth.

BEFORE making specific comments about the Federal-
State Employment Service, I'd like to put that Service in perspective against the national manpower picture. Virtually over-
night, manpower policy has become a dominating concern in
national and urban politics, and among economists, sociolo-
gists, psychiatrists, and private welfare organizations.

An unyielding high unemployment rate for young people,
triple that for adults, is a paramount reason. The youth rate
could worsen with the full coming of age of the wartime
babies. One million more youths will look for jobs in 1965 than
in 1964. This occurs as perhaps 40,000 jobs disappear per week
owing mainly to technological change, many of them so-called
entry jobs of the lower skill variety.

The Negro civil rights movement is another factor stimulating interest in the reformulation of our public and private manpower policies. This is increasingly true as the movement's
focus has shifted from public accommodations and housing to
jobs. The job is correctly seen as the key to social survival. Cut-

backs in the armaments-space complex, with consequent large
layoffs, further agitate manpower policy issues, and such cutbacks are scheduled to increase.

At least two other influences are directing greater attention
to manpower issues. There is a widely shared hunch that much
of today's social tension, most dramatically the riots by unemployed Negro youth, has to do with the breaking down of one
of history's oldest relationships, the relationship between income and work. The work-income nexus is threatened—this
when our economy is almost totally a job economy and is urban-
ized. It is threatened by the beginnings of what is called the
age of cybernation—that is, the linking of computers with
mechanized production, to replace man not only as producer
but also as operator. Meanwhile abundance increases, but not
new jobs. On the contrary. Hence we are seeing such notions as
the Ad Hoc Committee of the Triple Revolution's [1] uncondi-
tional guaranteed income. This latter idea does not seem very
bizarre when one considers that only a short time ago President
Johnson himself told the Communications Workers of America
in Cleveland that "I will take further steps to make sure that
every American who wants to work can work." One way or
another, income is to be guaranteed, it would seem. But man
may feel psychologically stranded as the old values seem to
crumble and the future appears so uncertain.

Finally—and this is the second influence I had in mind—we
are seeing the academicians increasingly emphasize the close
correlation between investment in manpower and a nation's
economic growth. This, too, is rousing greater interest in manpower questions. Dr. Walter Heller himself has said that our
devotion of resources to intangible human capital (education,

---

[1] A committee of economists, political scientists, and writers concerned with
structural unemployment, civil rights, nuclear holocaust, and overcentralized
government.

culture, research) has accounted for half our economic growth in the twentieth century. Professor Galbraith pleads for us to see educational expenditures as an *investment,* not as consumption which should be economized. Behind this thinking is the belated recognition that the older classic economic orthodoxy that labor is homogeneous, with all laborers assumed to be about equally endowed, is just not true. It follows from this that the upgrading of its manpower is a nation's cardinal economic mission.

In any event, it is against this new absorption with manpower policy that one must try to view the role of the Federal-State Employment Service. It is fashionable among academicians and those in the thick of manpower affairs to disdain the Service. I lament this lack of appreciation of its crucially important function, and I especially deplore the hostility toward the service by business. This is the underlying reason the Service is less effective than it could be.

There is a difficult problem here. Only if the business system uses the Service will it improve (i.e., job openings would be listed; workers would patronize it more regularly). But without some new kinds of inducements or leverages the Service is not likely to be used until it *is* deemed a better Service. So we have a kind of vicious circle.

And the public generally (94 percent of it more or less happily employed) doesn't much care because it shares the conventional notion that the labor market in our market economy has a self-regulating nature akin to the self-regulating character of the market itself. Were this assumption valid, then a tax cut, successfully stimulating the economy generally and nourishing demand and the requisite purchasing power, would melt away all hard-core unemployment.

What should have become evident, however, is that technological changes, and the fact that ours is now a highly developed mass consumption society making for inelasticity of demand, have changed the labor market so that it is much less responsive to over-all market forces than it used to be. The number and the kinds of job opportunities being created today and their location are very different from what they were only a few years ago, and they are more difficult to anticipate because of the rapidity and the complexity of change.

Well, the labor market isn't proving itself to be self-correcting, and hence the essentiality of the Employment Service in matching demand and supply in a complex, subtle, ever-changing continental (rather than local or regional) economy.

How can it be improved?

Here are some specific suggestions. I have just said there must be greater involvement of the business system, which after all is the fundamental dynamic force in our economy and the biggest employer. There should be inducements or leverages to involve business. For example, there is the critical matter of our ignorance of job vacancies. All government contractors should list their job openings (of the nonpromotion variety) with the Service. No one should have to pay a fee to get employment deriving from government business.

Furthermore, business firms generally might list their openings with the Service under the incentive of tax savings. Listing openings does *not* mean that the firm is also compelled to hire applicants sent by the Service. That can remain a voluntary matter. But the listing alone would act to upgrade the attractiveness of the Service to the work force, especially to clientele not claiming unemployment insurance. This in turn would enable the Service to perform more effectively for business generally, and in this manner the whole operation would become enhanced. As it is, if the Service is felt to know only about second-rate jobs and to handle only second-rate people, the whole system is obviously ignored.

The same principle of offering some kind of tax inducement could apply to another phase of activity of vital concern to a properly functioning employment service, namely the establishing of on-the-job training in private industry. Employers who have an approved on-the-job training operation would get a tax break; those who don't would in effect be penalized. In this day and age, there is depreciation in skills, too, and employees need protection from obsolescence.

Again, the same principle might be applied in connection with businesses that take the initiative to provide the Service with advance warning of employment changes, pre-eminently those caused by automation and technological change.

If all this sounds rather unbusinesslike, I refer you to the recent address before the 34th National Business Conference, at the Harvard Business School, by the Chairman of the Board of The Equitable Life Assurance Society of the United States, James F. Oates, Jr. Mr. Oates stated that the precedent for a tax incentive for hiring hard-core unemployed youth can be found in the investment credit for plant and equipment incorporated in the 1962 revenue bill. Said Mr. Oates, "I see no compelling reason why a similar tax credit could not be offered to employers who make payroll expenditures at the legal minimum rates for certain carefully defined classes of unskilled, marginal labor whose employment we seek to encourage."

In a word, I am suggesting that surely we have the ingenuity today to get the business system to cooperate actively with the Employment Service in making job vacancies known; in setting up on-the-job training; in providing jobs for those needing some kind of preferential treatment so that they can at least

matriculate into the labor force; and in encouraging advance
warning of layoffs.

With respect to training, it is well known that the best training and retraining is the on-the-job variety. It is less expensive
and more efficient, and it carries an overriding psychological
advantage to the trainee, who senses that this is for real, not
some schoolmaster's concoction.

Another point I would like to make is that the Service needs
better, more highly educated counselors, and it needs the
wherewithal to hold on to them. Counseling is crucial in this
day when—in contradiction to the older economic theory that
automation would mean only unskilled labor would be needed
to do the residue work—the demand for all kinds of high-skill
labor intensifies. But to get and keep good counselors, as well
as interviewers, takes money. This would be forthcoming if the
payroll tax of $\frac{3}{10}$ of one percent that now pays for both the unemployment insurance system and the Employment Service
were based on the modern wage scale. It now applies to the
first $3,000 of payroll, the same as in 1939 when that sum
amounted to over 95 percent of payroll. Now it is less than 60
percent of payroll. It should be raised to apply to perhaps the
first $4,000 or $4,500 of payroll.

Actually, when one considers that employment is crucial to
the over-all health of society, a good case could be made that
money from general revenue rather than from a payroll tax
alone might go to paying for the Service. The calculus of costs
is a subtle matter. The tolls of delinquency and crime and of
massive welfare programs, for example, are great social costs
that could be ameliorated by the effective reduction of hard-
core, structural unemployment.

Occupational rehabilitation, as we are discovering from such examples as the Norfolk case [2] under the MDTA and the efforts at literacy training as well as skill training, is going to be painfully costly, difficult, and lengthy. But it is also worth the price. In the long run, what alternative do we have?

Incidentally, in regard to counseling and other staff services and costs, I believe I am correct in observing that the United States Employment Service has fewer staff and offices relative to the size of the work force it serves than any other modern Western industrial nation. By extension, of course, I would add that in addition to acquiring increased and improved staff and better and more accessible offices, the Service should begin to use automatic data processing on a much larger scale. There is evidence that the Service's operations are often too slow and cumbersome and less accurate than they must be if they are to serve a mobile, continental labor force.

Again, in respect to the cost question, I believe the point frequently is overlooked that the dollar savings effected by the Service when it cuts down the unemployment interval between jobs by as much as a week or two is huge. Last year the Service placed 4 million individuals. If the jobless time of each of these workers was reduced by one week and his average weekly wage was $80, a total of $320 million was saved. That's a quite conservative estimate, not including the various savings in relief, unemployment benefits, etc.

I would like to conclude with these miscellaneous points:

The Service has suffered in the past and perhaps still suffers from its anxiety to "prove" itself to inquiring Congressmen and Senators, by showing an impressive mechanical production so as to justify appropriations. It has used a so-called performance

---

[2] The Norfolk Case refers to an instance of successful training of what had heretofore been considered "unemployables" in a project in Norfolk, Va., under an early MDTA program.

budget. This derived originally from the effort to justify the amount of staff handling unemployment insurance claims. This kind of work is relatively easy to quantify in the way that accountants prefer, based on the volume of transactions in a given unit of time. The Employment Service's adoption of this kind of performance budgeting has been harmful, because it militates against the very services that have become most important and are hardest to quantify—namely counseling, interviewing, and the more complex personal contacts needed to have a first-rate operation. They have shifted now to a so-called program budget, which is less satisfactory perhaps to accountants but is more realistic since it establishes staff and goals for budgeting on the basis of what services must be rendered on the criteria of quality and of human priorities.

It would be a calamity if the adversaries of the Service were somehow to succeed in having its scope restricted to the unemployed. The Service would be effectively killed because obviously it could not even serve the unemployed if it were to be so confined. The Service can only succeed to the extent that it is fully patronized by business and by the widest range of workers. This patronage would disappear if the Service were looked upon as dealing only with the relatively unqualified jobless, as it would be should such a restriction be imposed. The Service must accommodate the whole labor market if it is to work— including professionals, whose work orientation, incidentally, is becoming increasingly nation-wide and therefore demands nation-wide information that only the Service can command.

The anxieties of the private fee-charging employment agencies should be recognized as being both exaggerated and untempered by any anxieties about the public interest. They are exaggerated because there isn't the slightest prospect that their legitimate role will ever be taken away from them. Even in Sweden the public service accounts for at most 30 percent of placements. The American fee-charging industry has continued to grow and prosper. But there are a vast number of Americans —and they'll be more vast now that the passage of civil rights legislation will encourage them to aspire upward in their job careers—who are seeking to upgrade themselves vocationally. They are not considered desirable clients by the private agencies, and they can't afford those agencies. Moreover, they desperately need the kind of objective, comprehensive counseling, referral, and placement help the U.S. Employment Service can render if given the means to do so.

The 1963 amendments to the MDTA provide some $4 million for experiments in relocation assistance. Plans are being drawn up for a research program in South Bend, following the demise of the Studebaker operation there. This is encouraging but excessively timid when it is realized that immobility is a cardinal characteristic of the disadvantaged jobless. Given the increasingly rapid rate of change in our industrial order, it is inevitable that our resources for assisting in relocating the jobless will have to expand as our knowledge of the right techniques becomes more secure.

HELP WANTED

by Ivar Berg

Ivar Berg is Associate Professor at Columbia University Graduate School of Business, author of more than a dozen articles in scholarly publications, and coauthor of three books. He was a Woodrow Wilson Fellow in 1954–55, and a Chester Hastings Arnold Fellow in Contemporary Civilization at Harvard in 1955–56. He has served as advisor to the National Committee on Employment of Youth, the U. S. Department of Labor, the Carnegie Foundation, the State Farm Insurance Company, Western Electric Corporation, the Chemical Bank New York Trust Company, and IBM.

"YOUTH is such a wonderful thing," George Bernard Shaw once said, "what a crime it is to waste it on children." Today's statistics on unemployment among the young—particularly of minority groups—suggest a slight modification of the epigram. If we drop the last two words, it expresses an unfortunate truth about today's unemployment problem. The implications are even more unfortunate for the adults the young will become; in a society in which work and productivity are weights for measuring a man's worth, the innocent victims of joblessness will continue to be found wanting in the market place over their lifetimes.

Part of the problem no doubt resides in the personal shortcomings of the youths themselves. They must be armed with skills and ambitions if the "war on poverty" is to be properly waged. Educators, business leaders, and well-meaning candidates for public office are tireless in their promotion of education and training; and there is no dearth of programs designed to encourage and enable the young to complete their formal education, acquire diverse skills, and develop appropriate personal attributes. But those who make education and training the overriding issue are enlisting in the war on poverty to fight skirmishes against the poor and unemployed—not against the real enemy, which is the condition of unemployment. "Screaming at the kids" is sorry enough as a parental technique in child-rearing; as a social policy it is unthinkable.

To be sure, training and education programs will make many young people "employable," but only in the limited sense that they will come to the market place with the skills of those already favored with jobs. There they will have to compete in a race against others to fill an inadequate demand. The war in Vietnam has temporarily injected an artificial element into the demand for labor, a demand that failed to employ our manpower fully even before our wartime babies reached employment age. Teenagers have been deluded by the rest of us into believing that they control their own occupational destinies, and unless systematic efforts are made to provide many more jobs, training and education may only serve to embitter them as they grow older. Clearly, efforts must be made to alter the terms of the supply-and-demand equation by which we describe the operation of the market system. Efforts, that is, to create jobs.

In the current debate on unemployment and the strategies for creating jobs, liberals and conservatives, each in their own way, have focused on what the government should do. Neither camp has made much room for the exercise of private initiative, despite widespread commitments to that virtue, which Americans rank with motherhood.

Let us begin by considering the role of the government as many liberals see it. To them the first, and most obvious, solution to the problem of unemployment is public works. Some of them argue that public works should be conducted much as they were in the thirties, when the aim was to create jobs in combination with improving the cities and the countryside. Others, sensitive to the lingering image of workers leaning on shovels, would make public works at once less visible and more palatable to the taxpayer. Title I of the "Antipoverty Act" therefore calls for "residential vocational training" to be combined with conservation work in the forests. Whichever way we conceive of public works and how the government should formulate and implement them, the fact of the matter is that so long as our streets are littered, the parks blighted, and public buildings weathered; so long as urban transportation facilities are underequipped and abominably appointed, roads dented with axle-breaking potholes and parks woefully unattended, there are tasks to which people—young people—could be set.

The public works of the thirties were born of liberal minds and executed by liberal government officials who saw public work programs as part of an elaboration and extension of reforms calculated to make capitalism work. They sought not only to provide for needs that were not being met by private initiative, but to limit the sometimes perverse excesses of private enterprise, the gross inequalities in income distribution, and the occasionally wanton misuse of market power by unregenerate "captains of industry." But there is a new breed of liberals abroad in the land today. Their objectives are not new, but their tactics are novel and have important implications. The new breed is given to "understanding" the businessman, most of whom in the new view are basically not "malefactors of great wealth." With good advice and some help, businessmen are indeed benefactors of our economic health. "Understanding" is sometimes even coupled with outright praise. Leon H. Keyserling, when he was Chairman of President Truman's

Council of Economic Advisors, told a manpower symposium this fall that ". . . private enterprise has done a good job in becoming more and more efficient, and this necessarily eliminates jobs; therefore, they have to be created somewhere else." In his judgment and that of many others, we have benefited from the New Deal reforms and from the marvelous productivity of efficient private enterprise. The logic seems to be that we cannot expect reasonable business leaders to undertake to solve "residual" problems; these are in the province of the government and should be dealt with by a modest expansion of public housing ventures, urban renewal, school construction, road-building, and the expansion of health facilities.

Freed by liberals of responsibility for the side effects of efficiency and prosperity, and absolved of guilt for the deplorable condition of a fifth of the nation, the business community, it is thus presumed, could be brought around to recognizing the many public needs for educational, medical, recreational, and other facilities. The new liberals act as though the conscience of the conservative can be made absolvable by the heady flatteries of White House dinner invitations, and by sympathetic statements concerning the notorious "profit squeeze." One may recall, in this connection, that the business community did not receive even one ritual blast from any well-known Democrat in the last Presidential election campaign! But if some business statesmen and a few more citizens are congenial to the idea of sizable Federal outlays for public improvements, there are demonstrably many more who recoil from it.

There are real risks in the new liberal rhetoric, in that the businessman will gladly accept the absolutions without feeling any obligation to support a fast deal. It is unlikely that many who are close to our corporations—and aware of the inefficiencies, errors, waste, abuses of public trust, and the idle capacity that balance their very notable accomplishments—will be easily fired up to support public projects if at the same time they despair of fulfilling the promises of private enterprise.

A second solution to the problem of unemployment appears to focus on the private sector of the economy, the very sector the liberals praise with increasingly faint damns. The private sector must expand, and we hear a great deal about the need for "growth policies" from those who play at what I like to call the "confidence game." Job opportunities, according to the confidence theorists, are a by-product of economic growth, which in turn is the necessary product of a series of public postures and a few government policies. Generate confidence among businessmen and investors, theorists tell us, and jobs will follow; jobs coincide with economic growth, which is born of publicly "encouraged" but privately undertaken decisions.

Chief among the policies that will breed this vital confidence, according to the growth school, is the stabilization of government spending on nonessential (that is, nondefense) public works and welfare benefits. Note the word "stabilization." There is little call from the growth school for cutbacks on government contracts, publicly-financed "private" research, or subsidies to corporate activities. Not even all special-interest rulings by the government are discouraged. Little objection was raised to the decision by the Internal Revenue Service permitting the twenty-nine electrical equipment manufacturers who were convicted of defrauding customers in the pricing conspiracy trial of 1960 to deduct over $150 million in damages from their income tax as "ordinary and necessary business expenses." The figure may reach $300 million, a little less than half the amount finally appropriated for the Administration's war on poverty. According to the inexplicable, onesided logic of those who play the confidence game, growth policies are those that do not directly benefit no-income or low-income population groups; "social welfare" policies are those that do serve these groups. Corrupting and immoral dependency on aid in the one group is initiative in response to opportunity in the other. It calls to mind John Lothrop Motley's epicurean paradox: "Give us the luxuries of life, and we will dispense with its necessaries."

But it is not necessary to refute the theory of growthmanship with logic. Let us instead allow that stabilization of government spending will encourage the growth of private enterprise. Let us further allow that the government could be less heavy-handed in its regulation of industry, could exercise a lighter hand on the tax lever, could discipline the nocturnal visitations of its F.B.I. agents, could establish fewer "guideposts," and make a little less of its antitrust powers. Let us even concede that if confident private planners will invest and produce more, the commonweal will thereby be promoted. The need for jobs remains, confidence-inspiring policies notwithstanding. There is no denying that the economy has grown and that its growth has been sustained. The bribes that are euphemistically dubbed growth policies have worked to an extraordinary degree; tax cuts, depreciation allowances, and subsidies have played their part in increasing the number of jobs in our economy. At the same time we have learned to produce more of everything, increasing the gross national product figure yearly. But our population is also increasing. Half a million youths entered the work force between 1950 and 1960. More than eleven times as many will enter in the present decade. We thus have economic growth and rising profits without a corresponding rise in employment.

Private entrepreneurs have many options for mixing labor with other resources, as they have for earning profits. An ad-

vertisement in a recent issue of the Harvard Business Review
declares that "There is as much profit in a 1.5 percent purchasing saving as in a 10 percent sales increase" at today's average
profit margins. With approximately 12 percent of our physical
plant standing idle, the choice between such options could be
significant. While it is possible to rationalize decisions in what
are supposedly value-free economic terms, the choices made
may have profound social and moral implications. Higher sales
might require higher production rates and in some instances
more workers, while cuts in purchases could affect the quality
and attractiveness of a product. In fairness to the ad, one might
hope that we would cut costs and sell more so as to call out at
least the efficient portion of our idle capacity. United States
Steel, after years of what many conversant with the steel industry called arrogant pricing and sluggish promotion, has recently responded to long-neglected opportunities. The sleepy
giant has begun to stir and even some of its more obsolete
plants have recently been called back into action. We may
hope that while Big Steel (because of its price policies) can
make a profit even when less than half of its resources are in
use, it will choose to continue to make money and jobs. Growth
policies, however, do not guarantee both outcomes; they do not
oblige corporations to sell harder.

There are very few strings tied to the costly package of
benefits afforded corporations by the public. A company that
has made "foolish" investments earns the same depreciation allowances for writing off its obsolete equipment as a company
that has planned carefully. The energetic company is eligible
for no more subsidy than the ineffective company with outmoded marketing techniques. The costs of harboring unemployed youth, meanwhile, are not low, whatever the corporation may save by laying off personnel. We spend tax money on

the unemployed; we lose their productivity and their taxes. The unemployed themselves lose hope, dignity, often health, and usually all sense of identity with the society that cuts them off. The waste all around is incalculable.

If public spending requires popular support that is difficult for liberals to mobilize so long as it provokes antagonism among the lieutenants of bureaucratic industry, and if growth policies simply modify "profitless prosperity" in favor of "jobless profitability," what then are the alternatives?

Some business managers—a small but growing number—are finding places for unemployed youth by hiring in excess of their immediate needs. The Equitable Life Assurance Society, Bloomingdale's department store in New York, the Illinois Bell Telephone Company, and Hallmark Cards are among them. In some instances the youths are trained for extended periods and then sent out into the economy to fill vacant jobs in other companies that are short of the skills the newly trained have acquired. In other instances the youths are kept in the work forces of the companies where they trained, while older employees are upgraded to fill vacancies further up the hierarchy of skills. If the steel industry had been doing the same, it might not have found itself faced with the shortage of highly skilled workers this fall.

Companies attempting to act on rather than react to our employment problems have chosen from among various policies. The nature, duration, costs, and achievements differ from corporation to corporation. Indeed, as the steel illustration implies, it is often difficult to gauge between the short- and long-run costs of manpower policies. The important thing to note is that, whatever their details, these programs represent an effort to meet the problem. While they are by no means a substitute for successful and acceptable applications of welfare spending for poor and rich, these programs can help reduce the magnitude of the unemployment problem, thus helping us to win some time and save some lives.

The fact is that in all of these "youth-serving" employment programs in the private-sector hands have been hired in excess of needs.

The idea is not revolutionary. There have been other times when industries have maintained work forces in excess of short-term needs. During World War II, shipyards were fully manned between contracts. To be sure, government contracts, with their guarantees for recovering costs, helped foot the bill. But there were economies accruing from the stable work force. If a peacetime application were to be made of such arrangements, it would be necessary for a corporation to increase orders to keep the shops going as government contracts once did; in a society with unused capacity, one company's new orders do not necessarily come at the expense of another's, and the added national product would provide some jobs. President Eisenhower and his Secretary of Commerce said as much when they suggested that automobile dealers, spoiled by a postwar sellers' market, get out from under their Rotary Club plaques in their pine-paneled offices to ring doorbells. This is not so easy as waiting for a "cost-plus" contract, but it is more attractive than paying the unemployment bill.

If it be argued that wartime is special, consider the printing industry. Years ago the newspapers began to hire extra personnel in advance of the busy hour when they went to press. To offset the costs, they found additional tasks to occupy their expensive typographers over a full workday; advertising and much other copy began to be set over a rationally planned time period, and the practice has continued to the present.

In other industries, young trainees and employees could

render additional services that would undoubtedly be wel-
comed by customers, and might even profit their employers.
The long lines of customers awaiting the attention of harried
personnel at cash registers, refund counters, and credit desks
are a familiar sight on the suburban shopping scene. Delays in
apartment repairs add to the irritations and inconveniences of
city living. Consumer journals and the Federal Trade Commis-
sion report on hastily assembled, faultily packaged, and incom-
pletely outfitted consumer products, provide abundant testimony to the need for care that additional personnel might give.

The benefits of extra hiring would not be limited to management and the customers; the employees themselves would
profit. With all the changes wrought by a generation of enlightened managers and alert trade union leaders, there are still
too many laborers in America who work strenuous eight-hour
stints at heavy and repetitive tasks. In our mass-production industries, there are instances where relief time is contractually
guaranteed but where relief personnel are too few to permit
predictable breaks to serve basic needs. The recent strikes in
the automobile industry are instructive; union leaders were no
less upset than managers by striking auto workers in some
plants who rejected attractive national settlements on wages
and other economic goodies for want of more fundamental
human comforts.

Consider the case of Rich Piechowski, a mechanic in Detroit
who climbs into an auto body once every 58 seconds to install
pads around the base of the steering column. He was pleased
beyond middle-class comprehension at the settlement of the
last contract, which allows him 32 minutes' relief time per
eight-hour shift, an addition of twelve minutes over the provision of the earlier agreement. "A trip to the washroom or a
fast cup of coffee four times a shift will make me feel a little

human again," he said to an interviewer after the agreement
had been reached this fall. The logic of efficiency makes no
room for such preindustrial considerations; after all, labor is
expensive. Is it not possible, however, to envision room for a
youth or two on a line of which 62 cars per hour roll past a man
who needs only four eight-minute breaks to "feel a little human
again"?

Although the idea of an "excess of manpower" is not new and
the possibilities for extensions of service are evident, the objections are many. The objections have a grand history; they
derive from orthodox economic thought. But let us consider
them in the forms they took in 1959, the year of the Great Steel
Strike.

The first cousin to augmenting a work force by hiring dropouts "not needed" by a firm is the practice of retaining a given
work force when technological changes make some employees
"redundant." Cases of such practices were trotted out before
the public in 1959 and labeled "Luddite attitudes" (after the
early nineteenth-century artisans who destroyed textile machines in the English midlands) and condemned as "wasteful
featherbedding" sought by lazy blue-collar workers and their
irresponsible labor leaders. The steel dispute of 1959 left most
Americans, easily inspired by their atavistic puritanism anyway, shocked at the rampant waste in our economy. Business
firms were portrayed as helpless victims of the market and the
unions, which were said to be unresponsive to the challenges
that faced America. This, despite the fact that work rules were
established by bargaining procedures in the shop and in formal
negotiations in which (we may hope!) alert managers obtained
something of value—an extra function performed, a lower
wage demand, an opportunity to change a mechanical proce-
dure, a willingness to meet a revised shipping schedule—in exchange for the work rules they conceded.

Overlooked by the editorial writers, business journalists, economy-minded politicians, and Reader's Digest savants who condemned the concessions were the advantages to the firm of the exchanged values; they did not look beyond the "oversized crews," "too-slow production lines," "unfair rates," and "excessively low standards" when they condemned as nefarious the rules that seemed to nurture inefficiency. Only a few reminded us that the questions "How big is big?" "How fast is fast?" and "How reasonable is reasonable" were unanswerable, though not unbargainable. Arthur J. Goldberg, then the steelworkers' counsel, suggested as much in a different way at the last of the fact-finding committees convened by President Eisenhower in the closing days of the eighty-day injunction that stopped the strike. "We reject the companies' last offer," he said, "for it reads: 'Work rules will be changed in the interest of efficiency with due regard for employees'; we feel that the statement should be reversed so that it reads: 'Work rules will be changed in the interest of employees with due regard for efficiency.'"

This brief discussion of work rules and efficiency is very much to the point in appraising policies for hiring extra personnel. According to a report in the *Wall Street Journal* (January 3, 1964), 60,000 jobs—the equivalent of slightly less than 10 percent of the teenagers currently seeking work—would result if America's 100 largest corporations took on the equivalent of one percent of their payrolls. It will be argued that hiring "excess workers" may be a fine thing for a few affluent corporations to undertake, but few companies could seriously consider doing so. In support of this argument there will be a predictable array of negative reasons couched in the familiar economic and psychological terms used in the steel strike and in the frequent attacks on "social welfare" legislation.

First, there is sure to be emphasis placed on the term "excess," as though there were clear lines indicating how much a person or persons should do; then the objection will be entered that payrolls are based on the parameters, however arbitrary, according to which a firm must operate to compete with others. But cost data are hard to come by, as labor leaders and investigation-bent Senators will testify. We do know that price competition, in connection with which labor costs are often relevant, has given way in both rhetoric and reality to non-price competition in many industries. Industrial as well as retail consumers are made attentive to differences in product quality, to services, to quick delivery dates, and to the other criteria by which products are differentiated. Daniel Bell has deftly juxtaposed the incomplete data on automobile pricing as disclosed in Congressional hearings with additional, but also incomplete, information contained in the recent autobiography of Alfred P. Sloan of General Motors, and concluded that automobile prices are set in such a way that they will return a profit after a break-even point has been passed, which in turn is based on cost calculations from the lowest sales year in a five-year period.[1] When the company enjoys record-breaking sales—higher by far than the sales of the year used for determining cost data—it enjoys substantial profits to the degree that economies of scale are operative and unit costs thereby reduced from those in the low sales years used in price calculations. In the steel industry the break-even figure is reliably reported to be reached when 48 percent of capacity is in use. Presumably prices could reflect the economies that set in when higher levels of production are achieved. While we may envy and even approve of a company's good fortune in being able to get top prices for their products, we wonder about "high labor costs" in industries

[1] Daniel Bell, in *The New York Review of Books*, III, No. 2 (Sept. 10, 1964), p. 12.

whose labor costs go down with higher levels of production but appear to remain remarkably stable in discussions about job opportunities and labor costs. Better data are needed to evaluate industrial costs at different levels of production before we can accept economic arguments uncritically. This is especially true in our economy, when price competition is far from perfect in industries led by a comparatively few very large corporations capable of influencing the play of traditional market forces by virtue of their considerable size.

On the psychological issue it is argued, by Paul Jacobs and other liberals as well as by business leaders, that youth will be demeaned by what they call "make-work" policies.[2] But such arguments begin by assuming what instead they ought to prove: that there is no work to share. Second, foundation-financed journalists and academic entrepreneurs like Mr. Jacobs —who have abundant time for leisure, debate, and unhurried breaks—exaggerate the evil of youthful disenchantment with reduced work loads, when in many instances the young are totally idle outside our factory gates and office doors. Conservatives, by contrast, with a sense of morality that is quaint indeed, shudder at the thought of "extra hands" while they manage to look with equanimity on Appalachia.

While considering policies in the private sector we are obliged to note the argument, appearing with increasing frequency (especially in the business press), that there is a shortage of skilled workers, technicians, and engineers. Even before the escalation of the war in Vietnam began to have its beneficent effect on employment possibilities for adult males, we read of job vacancies in the skilled ranks in the steel industry and elsewhere. Unfortunately, the press releases fail to explore

[2] Paul Jacobs, *Deadhorse and Featherbirds,* Occasional Pamphlet (Santa Barbara, California, Center for the Study of Democratic Institutions, 1962).

the reasons for the shortages. One may wonder why unskilled workers were not trained and upgraded against the day when an enterprise might have an expanded market for its product. And one may wonder about the managerial competence of those whose increasing devotion to "long-range business planning" has led them to see so little of the future.

At the same time one may ask whether the dramatic increase in educational requirements for jobs—requirements that militate against any expansion in opportunities for large numbers of our youth—can be justified. The loose labor market of recent years, according to the gratuitous assumptions of most employers, has afforded them the chance of improving the "quality" of their work forces. The jacking-up of formal educational requirements is thus rationalized; it is defended, further, by the argument that it is easier to promote those with higher education. But there is much evidence that many engineers are used as technicians and that few semiskilled or skilled workers experience mobility in their occupational settings.

There is little evidence, meanwhile, that there are empirical differences in performance, in a particular job category, between those with relatively more and those with relatively less formal education. Such studies as are available, including a large-scale study by Cornell University Medical School researchers, strongly suggest that when such groups are compared in respect to their productivity and other components of job performance, the lesser educated group appears to be decidedly more valuable to employers. Employers, in fine, may be deluding themselves and shortchanging their firms by a thoughtless failure to exercise more initiative in examining the consequences of their employment practices. More seriously, they give evidence of distorting the manpower picture and contributing to significant orders of misallocation in the distribution and utilization of manpower. The consequences include public policies—like those in the war on poverty—that do little to solve the basic problems of unemployed youths.

With private initiative, meanwhile, much can be accomplished. The stories of American businessmen who have converted a losing product into a winner are numerous if not well known. One company with a useless inventory of wallpaper cleaner that would not sell simply added dyes to the product, relabeled it "Pladough" and in two years sold several million dollars' worth of the material across toy counters. One would hope that American managers capable of rescuing unused wallpaper cleaner from the rubbish pile might with similar ingenuity salvage a few live youths from the human debris left over from progress and plenty.

It is in many ways remarkable that many more managers of many more firms have not undertaken to use their initiative on youth unemployment problems. It would not be inconsistent with all of the businessmen's Grand Old Polemic. Consider that they may find the emerging generation seeking (if not demanding) more and more government assistance—in other words, seeking the "social welfare" so many businessmen decry. The future of private enterprise, as managers and investors conceive of it, may well depend on the men devoted to and proud of the great corporations they now run—and on their aiding, now, the children of our society.

GOVERNMENT INCENTIVES TO INDUSTRY FOR HIRING YOUTH

by Howard J. Samuels

Howard J. Samuels, Vice President of the Mobil Chemical Company and an industrial engineer, is an active advocate of the use of modern business techniques in government. Among his many civic affiliations, he is Chairman of the Citizens Committee for an Effective Constitution in New York State, a member of the U. S. Department of Labor Employment Service Task Force, and a Trustee of the Public Education Association. His pamphlet, *An Insufficient House,* outlines a massive education assistance program involving new principles of planning and financing.

ANY discussion of a subject such as "government incentives to industry for hiring youth" must begin by defining the scope and assumptions implicit in the topic. First, scope: We are not dealing here with young people in general, for such a discussion would encompass well-motivated, well-educated youngsters as well as those who are voluntarily unemployed; instead, the group we are concerned with is the *involuntarily unemployed* teenager who, for whatever reason, is unable to find a job. His unemployment and our political response to it necessitates an understanding of both the causes of his failure to move easily into the world of work, and the realities of what devices can be created to change that situation within the framework of our economic life.

Second, assumptions: The current emphasis at work in the Federal government is rehabilitation of people for the labor market. Increased public works, area redevelopment, manpower training, and the entire approach to Appalachia are examples of efforts in this direction. Indeed, the very topic we are discussing assumes that the government can do even more. But it makes one further assumption which is that if the right buttons are pressed by government, industry will respond and solve all of the problems.

I have great faith in our industrial genius and in the sincerity of business leaders to help with these problems, but I must state at the outset that I believe it is a great mistake to expect government incentives to business to be a major factor in solving the youth crisis in America, for two reasons.

The first reason is that there is a faulty premise underlying most discussions centering on this direction for the solution to youth unemployment, and that is that American industry will be altruistic at any cost. This is simply not realistic. Unless we face squarely the one constant fact of our economic life, which is that industry is in business to make a profit, ours will be no more than an exercise in rhetoric. There are things that can be done, but when we come to discuss them we must reduce to the simplest form two underlying facts and keep them in the forefront: Whatever incentives or appeals are made to industry, these must—I repeat, must—serve industry's profit motive; and the involuntarily unemployed young today are the least trained and least skilled of all unemployed. The present low level of their productivity must be faced, and their present skills evaluated toward the end of finding some way to make industry want to hire them while at the same time making it profitable to do so.

The second reason is our failure to come to grips with well-known facts of where job opportunities of the future will lie. Discussions of government incentives to industry appear to overlook the fact that employment in government and all other services is expected to increase between 1960 and 1975 at a rate almost double that of goods-producing industries.

If employment projections are to be taken seriously, the future for our young is in service industries and the public sector.

Population growth and the movement of people from rural to urban areas and to the suburbs will continue to expand the need for educational and health services, police and fire protection, sanitation, streets and highways, etc. Indeed, all across-the-board the projections by the U.S. Department of Labor are that the number of white-collar workers in general will grow more than twice as fast as the number of blue-collar workers from 1960 to 1970. Even now the great paradox in America is that there are 750,000 to 1 million youth who are unemployable while there is a need in our society for 750,000 to 1 million teachers, nurses, and other specialized technicians. This is the real wealth waste in the American society.

While we have this increasing need in service fields on one hand, on the other the reality is that American manufacturing has not produced one new net job in ten years. When we recognize that industry has spent more for research in the past eight years than in all the preceding years since 1900, we can predict a further decrease in manufacturing opportunities due to automation and technological change. Indeed, it has been estimated that 40,000 jobs a week are being eliminated by automation.

Although the jobs made obsolete so far have been mainly those performed by unskilled workers, the trend is increasingly in the direction of having both semiskilled and skilled jobs replaced by automated equipment. We ought seriously to consider whether we are on the right track in focusing on industry and how it can solve the youth employment problem, when we see in the midst of this alarming unemployment that there are tens of thousands of job openings for men and women *with the proper training*.

Perhaps there is no better indicator of the basic deficiency in education than the fact that the armed services are rejecting scores of young men as untrainable for military service. One out of every two selective service registrants called for pre-induction examinations are found unqualified, and it has been estimated that one-third of all young men in the nation turning eighteen would be found unqualified for either physical or mental reasons if they were to be examined for induction into the armed forces. The armed forces offer valuable opportunities to young persons to acquire many of the civilian skills needed in today's labor market. Countless jobs in the military service involve duties requiring craft or technical training; electronics, aircraft maintenance; automotive mechanics and metal working. Yet the benefits available from such training are limited to a relatively small number of young men who are able to meet the physical and mental standards for military service. If our armed services, which not only have the capacity for basic skill training and the ability to provide discipline unavailable to industry, find it uneconomical to accept the unemployables, isn't it a paradox that government should turn to industry and expect that some inducements could be found to stimulate mass hiring of the unemployables in the private sector?

The conclusion that forces itself upon us is that the youths that are unemployable are unemployable because they lack either basic formal education or motivation to stay in school. The challenge of the need for skilled people requires a new appreciation of the role and importance of education.

American society after the Civil War decided that basic education and motivation were most effectively and efficiently dealt with by the public sector and not the private sector of our nation.

I submit that we are on the threshold of so great a crisis that as a society we must make a new commitment: a massive commitment to finance general education on an unprecedented scale—a program which would involve the responsibility of society for educating the child of three rather than beginning at age five, and continuing until age seventeen or eighteen rather than permitting youngsters of sixteen to drop out of school.

The crisis facing American youth is deep. The reality is that American industry is ill-prepared to provide the basic education and motivation that are the *sine qua non* for solving the youth crisis in America. Many of us in the business world are beginning to recognize that wide-scale government action to develop and educate our human resources is a major factor in the growth of our free-enterprise system.

I recognize that the foregoing proposals are more in the nature of a broad, long-range scheme for uprooting the causes of the plight of our youth; however, I could not begin to discuss some of the current thinking on specific government incentive devices without this perspective, for the proposals I am about to discuss are no more than stopgap measures which do not involve any long-range solutions for youth unemployment and must only be regarded as temporary aids while we immediately undertake a new massive approach to education.

I would now like to shift attention to a discussion of other factors that may be contributing to large-scale unemployment among the young and some of the plans which have been presented as potential incentives for industry to hire youth. I think it is quite obvious from my previous discussion that I am less than optimistic that incentive plans can make more than a small dent in the problem.

The first of these suggestions has to do with subsidies of the unemployables. This approach underlies the programs designed to carry out the provisions of the MDTA and the various programs that make up much of the Administration's antipoverty war. The theory appears to be that since unemployables are uneconomic to industry, they will be made economic during an on-the-job training period by a direct subsidy to industry to use them. Proponents of this approach seem to see this as a method by which otherwise unemployable people can gain initial entry into industry, which would then continue their training in specific skills. It might be that another motive of the subsidy approach is to decrease the incentive of industry to invest in labor-saving devices through what amounts to a technique of featherbedding.

A logical extension of the existing policy of payments to industry is a proposal currently being advanced by a leader of industry, James F. Oates, Jr., Chairman of The Equitable Life Assurance Society of the United States.[1] He suggests a plan of direct subsidies either in the form of tax credits or in the form of payroll subsidies to employers who offer jobs to unskilled and untrained young people at legal minimum wage rates. He finds that there is precedent for tax credits in the investment credit incorporated in the 1962 revenue act, and that there is an analogy to payroll subsidies in the Federal agricultural price support policy. Both of these proposals merit consideration, particularly the open and direct payroll subsidy idea, which Oates points out has the advantage of creating new taxpayers out of the newly employed.

Yet despite the potential value of extension of the subsidy approach, it must be remembered that any massive undertaking of something like the payroll subsidy plan would of neces-

[1] Another speaker in this Symposium, Mr. Chase, has quoted Mr. Oates in this context.

sity eat into already overextended government budgets
financed out of current revenues. We know as a practical matter that the budgets for the current Federal subsidy programs
are only able to meet a fraction of the potential need, and even
these funds are not generally available to programs for young
people. For example, because of complicated administrative
criteria, only 25 percent of the funds administered through
MDTA programs are available to teenagers. There is no reason
to believe that there could be any more funds allocated for a
massive payroll subsidy plan for the young.

If these reflections seem pessimistic, there is yet another factor which may be a stumbling block to the young. That is the
subject of whether there may be some correlation between
massive youth unemployment and the state and national minimum wage laws, as many economists and business leaders are
beginning to suspect. It would appear that at this stage those
who are giving serious consideration to what can be done to
make jobs available to the young are pursuing a useful line of
inquiry in this subject. Minimum wage laws have played an
historical role in the American economy. They have eliminated
many labor abuses in the past and continue to be advocated
and expanded in the interest of employee welfare. Yet there a
negative effect seems unavoidable because of the nature of
what minimum wage laws actually do to the economy. If one
bears in mind the two factors mentioned earlier, namely the
low productivity of the young and industry's constant underlying motive to make profits, it follows that when society establishes not an economic wage, but rather a socially acceptable
wage, it tends to eliminate from consideration those who are
not worth the rate established for the enterprise. Moreover,
industry is inspired to find ways to reorganize and combine
jobs, or to replace them with machines in the process of keeping their prices competitive and their businesses operating

profitably. The minimum wage may thus in some cases constitute a nullifying effect to whatever good might come of Federal
subsidy programs which I suggested might be at least partially
designed to encourage featherbedding by lessening the economic hardship on industry to hire unprofitable people. I am
far from suggesting that minimum wage laws be eliminated, but
what I am suggesting is that the laws continue to be studied with
an eye to their impact on youth unemployment.

No less an authority than Professor George Stigler, President
of the American Economic Association, has been urging that
the economic well-being of a young boy could be improved by
lowering his wage rate to one dollar, for he points out how
much better to have raised his wage from zero to one dollar!
Such a stopgap measure, coupled with support grants for vocational education comparable to the G.I. Bill of Rights and a
continuation of welfare allowances, might well be considered
along with the other interim subsidy measures in an attempt to
get more young unemployables into the marketplace.

I return to my beginning, that the subsidy schemes in effect
and those being advocated, as well as the other programs
aimed at the broader unemployment crisis such as ARA and
the Appalachian project, though helpful and important to be
continued, cannot uproot the illness that may destroy our nation from within. The entire momentum of our technological
life is making it increasingly more difficult to survive without
basic skills created by a flexible education.

As long as we understand that these government incentives
to industry deal only with the *results* of the unemployment
problem of the young rather than with the *causes*, they may be
worth trying. None of these subsidy schemes, however, replaces the basic need for formal education, which is the responsibility of the public sector.

There is a mutually exclusive motivation between the short-range profit orientation of American business and the type of patient motivation and training required for the generation that has been passed by in economic life. I firmly believe that America's best long-range interests are served by keeping industry out of dealing with human problems that do not serve the profit incentive. The profit incentive has been and must continue to be the driving force in our free-enterprise society, and given a labor force equipped by training and motivation to mount the first rung of the business ladder we will be on the way to a full-employment economy.

JOB-CREATING POTENTIALS IN THE PUBLIC SECTOR

by Leon H. Keyserling

Leon H. Keyserling took a leading part in drafting government legislation between 1933 and 1953 in the fields of social security, banking and credit, public works and relief, and trade regulation. A frequent speaker and the author of numerous economic studies, he is now a consulting economist and attorney in Washington, D. C., and President of the Conference on Economic Progress. This article was excerpted from *Two Top-Priority Programs to Reduce Unemployment,* published by the Conference on Economic Progress, Washington, D.C.

DESPITE an economic "recovery" now said to be one of the "longest" on record, unemployment rose during the first eleven months of 1963, and in November 1963 was higher than during the corresponding periods of 1962. The true level of unemployment is now about 7 million. About 3¼ million, equating with full-time unemployment as officially reported of about 2 million, would be consistent with the prime national objective of maximum employment under the Employment Act of 1946. This true level of unemployment includes full-time unemployment, the full-time equivalent of part-time unemployment, and unemployment of those not counted as such because the shortage of jobs has discouraged their looking for work.

Unemployment is not an insoluble problem. It can be cured, and cured only by bringing total demand for ultimate goods and services into line with our increasing ability to produce them under the new technology and automation. Under the

American system, this is a task for both responsible free enterprise and responsible free government. But both are neglecting
the task, and failing to recognize their inescapable relationship.

Private enterprise, instead of initiating the steps which it can
and should take, is waiting to see what the government will do.

The government is permitting an "economy drive" to snow-
ball to such an extent that our native concern about the unemployed, the poor, and the deprived may become frozen in an
icy indifference.

THE PRIVATE ENTERPRISE AREA

The main default on the private enterprise side has been a failure to maintain a satisfactory balance between the flow of
funds into investment in the plant and equipment which add to
our productive capabilities, and the flow of funds which add to
the ability of consumers to buy enough to keep the plants fully
running and the manpower fully employed. This explains how
each short period of sharp economic upturn has been converted into stagnation, and how each stagnation prior to the
current one has been converted into recession. During the current stagnation since the fourth quarter of 1961, our average
annual growth rate has been less than 4 percent, or less than
half that required for at least two years to lift us from where
we are now to maximum employment and production. And
during this current stagnation, profits have soared to higher
levels than investors can use; investment in plant and equipment has once again expanded faster than demand for ultimate
goods and services; and consumer purchasing power has continued to lag seriously.

CENTRAL IMPORTANCE OF WAGE DEFICIENCIES

For 1963 estimated as a whole, a consumer spending deficiency
of about $59 billion has been more than three-quarters of the

total national production "gap" of $76.5 billion. Meanwhile, a $56.4 billion deficiency in wages and salaries has been more than three-quarters of the total personal income deficiency of $72.9 billion, which explains the inadequate consumer spending.

The chronically growing wage deficiency results largely because the hourly wage rates of those employed have lagged far behind productivity gains or increased output per man-hour worked. Until the huge shortage in purchasing power resulting from this is remedied, adequate reduction of unemployment remains impossible. During the five-year period 1957–62, while productivity in the whole private nonfarm economy rose at an average annual rate of 2.7 percent, real hourly earnings rose at an average annual rate of only 2.1 percent. In manufacturing, while productivity rose at an average annual rate of 3.4 percent, real hourly earnings rose at an average annual rate of only 1.8 percent. These vast disparities are augmenting even now.

The largest single step toward economic restoration needs to take the form of increases in hourly wage rates, to catch up with productivity gains and to reflect the accelerating rate of productivity gains under the new technology and automation. Starting with 1963 as a base, wages and salaries need to rise (through rate increases and reemployment) by about $72 billion by 1966, and by $160 billion by 1970.

THE SHORTER WORKWEEK

Hourly wage rates can be lifted either by maintaining the current length of the standard workweek and increasing weekly take-home pay, or by shortening the length of the standard workweek to thirty-five hours or thereabouts while maintaining the weekly take-home pay. Neither of these alternatives would be "inflationary" in terms of the increased demand for goods and services which they would generate, in view of the immense shortage of such demand now and in the foreseeable future. Neither of these alternatives should be set aside on the ground that it would "force up prices." Profit margins are now too high, and a better balance between funds available for investment and funds available for consumption would expedite economic growth, reduce idle manpower and plant, and enhance aggregate profits and investment in the long run. And in view of the fact that with the current standard workweek no dent in unemployment is foreseeable under private and economic policies now under active consideration, a shorter workweek appears manifestly desirable.

LABOR'S ADAPTABILITY TO CHANGES IN DEMAND

It is frequently said that the high unemployment of today is largely attributable to the lack of preparation of a substantial part of the labor force for the available types of jobs. Of course, there is always need for programs to educate, train and retrain, and relocate workers. But every period of reasonably full employment—above all the World War II period—has taught us that fitting the worker to the job is a relatively minor problem when the jobs are there. Many workers are trained on the job, and we cannot know what kind of jobs to train people for until the jobs are available or are being made available. Furthermore, the general and widespread nature of high unemployment makes it very clear that the main trouble is the shortage of total jobs, rather than the unadaptability of the labor force. Thus, if the composition and structure of demand receive due attention, the structure of the labor force will adjust itself without great difficulty.

But adjustments within the structure of private enterprise cannot do the whole expansionary job. First, the size of the job is
too big and the need for speed too urgent. Second, the rates of
technological advance and automation in various industrial
sectors and in agriculture are moving so much faster than any
feasible expansion of consumer needs and wants in these areas,
that it will be impossible to restore maximum employment by
increases in purchasing power directed solely at goods and
services produced in industry and agriculture. A large proportion of the structure of total demand must be redirected to
those types of goods and services which require new admix-
tures of private and public spending, with a heavy accent upon
increased Federal spending. Third, only this increased public
spending can fill some of the top priorities of our unmet national needs. These include, among others, rehousing of slum
dwellers and renewal of our urban areas; enlargement of educational, health, and recreational facilities and services; improvements in mass transportation; and expansion of resource
development and conventional types of public works.

Restoration and maintenance of maximum employment and
production require, as we have noted, much larger increases in
Federal outlays than are now under consideration. This crucial
point requires summation.

First, a $4.2 billion average annual deficiency in Federal
goods and services outlays, especially taking account of the
"multiplier" effects of Federal spending, has been a very important factor in the chronic rise of unemployment and idle plant
during the period 1953–63.

Second, a balanced model for restoration and maintenance of
maximum employment and production requires that Federal

public outlays for goods and services be lifted above the calendar 1963 level by $13 billion in calendar 1966, and $27 billion in calendar 1970.

Third, very large increases in public employment are needed to make the structure of employment responsive to technological trends, to the changing pattern of the people's wants, and to the priorities of our national needs.

Fourth, the required rapid expansion of some of the types of private employment hinges upon large increases in public outlays. The huge projected expansion of employment in contract construction, especially housing and urban renewal, depends upon a vigorous admixture of additional private and public spending. The large projected expansion of private employment in the services category, especially in education, health, and recreation, calls for much more Federal assistance for building facilities and recruiting and training personnel.

SPECIFICS OF THE NEED

The specific goals for the Federal Budget include: education, where per capita outlays (measured in 1962 dollars) should be lifted from $7.87 in fiscal 1964 to $32.86 by calendar 1970; health services and research, where Federal per capita outlays over the same period of time should be lifted from $8.41 to $22.54; public assistance, where the lift should be from $15.48 to $21.13; labor and manpower, and other welfare services, where the lift should be from $4.85 to $5.63; and housing and community development, where the lift should be from $1.42 to $15.49. For all domestic programs and services, Federal per capita outlays should be lifted from $186.83 to $239.44. All this allows for a lift in per capita Federal outlays for national defense, space technology, and all international assistance, from $319.03 to $396.71.

Including other needs such as national resource development and conventional types of public works, the total Federal Budget should be lifted from $98.8 billion as originally proposed by the Administration for fiscal 1964 to $115 billion by calendar 1966, and $135.5 billion by calendar 1970. In an economy growing at the rate which these outlays would help to induce, total Federal outlays as a percent of total national production would decline considerably, and the total national debt as a percent of total national production would decline greatly.

The time to start moving on these increased Federal outlays is now. The intolerable levels of unemployment and idle plant demands it; the needs of the people require it; and ordinary economic prudence calls for it. As a first step, it was recommended that outlays for domestic purposes in the Federal Budget for fiscal 1965, presented in January 1964, be $3.5 to $4 billion higher than those originally presented for fiscal 1964. Allowing for built-in increases, and desirable expansion in some other areas including assistance overseas and space research and technology, the total Federal Budget for fiscal 1965 ought to be $8 to $8.5 billion higher than the original Budget for 1964, or about $107 billion.

TAX REDUCTION NO SUBSTITUTE
FOR FEDERAL SPENDING

Tax reduction, by placing more spendable income in the hands of consumers, will increase demand for many types of production. But any feasible increases in conventional demand, combined with the rates of advance in technology and automation in the industries where these products are being turned out, do not offer reasonable promise of contributing a major portion of the estimated 22.5 million additional jobs required over the next decade (about one-half net additions, and about one-half needed in place of jobs eliminated by technology and automation). Nor can tax reduction alone make a major contribution to many of the highest priorities of our national public needs.

Greatly accelerated housing and urban renewal would be the largest single opportunity to direct increased Federal spending toward a solution of the basic problems defined just above. This would activate maximum increases in private employment and private investment for every dollar of increased public spending, and through resulting increases in tax revenues would combine these needed increases in Federal spending with an optimum long-range program to reduce greatly and ultimately to eliminate the Federal deficit.

For 1963, new nonfarm housing starts are estimated by $1.6 million. But practically all of this serves middle- and high-income groups, and so it has been in years gone by. This recurrently saturates the market. It leads to the extraordinary instability of housing starts, which contributes to general economic instability. It furnishes inadequate expansion of employment opportunity. It makes only picayune progress toward helping the one-fifth of the nation who are still ill-housed.

The Conference on Economic Progress has therefore proposed a new long-range housing effort, very large in size and scope, starting at once and running through 1970. The program is pointed toward 2 million new nonfarm housing starts in 1966, and 2.2 million in 1970, divided as follows: (1) about 1.2 million units in 1966 and in 1970 of conventionally financed private housing for middle- and high-income families; (2) about 0.4 million units in 1966 and about 0.5 million in 1970 for lower-middle income families; this would be privately financed housing, but with Federal assistance directed toward lower interest rates, longer amortization terms, and aid to land assembly and other aspects of urban renewal; and (3) about 0.4 million units in 1966 and about 0.5 million in 1970 for low-income families who now live in slums, with Federal subsidy assistance as well as state and local assistance.

LOW FEDERAL COSTS IN TERMS OF BENEFITS

The proposed program would require that the item in the Federal Budget for housing and community development (urban renewal) be lifted from about $250 million in fiscal 1964 to $2.2 billion in calendar 1966 and $3.3 billion in calendar 1970. Even with these lifts, these outlays would comprise less than 3 percent of the Federal Budget in 1970 and only 0.37 percent of what our total national production should be by that year.

Federal outlays for these purposes—$3 billion higher in calendar 1970 than in fiscal 1964—would contribute powerfully to a projected increase of almost $23 billion in private residential nonfarm construction in 1970, compared with calendar 1963. This in turn would contribute powerfully to a projected increase of about $40 billion in private investment in total new construction. Coordinately with this, employment in contract construction (of which employment in residential construction should be an increasingly large part), measured from a 1962 base, should and can be lifted 37.8 percent by 1966 and 48.6 percent by 1970, contrasted with a lift in total civilian employment (from a 1962 base) of 13.4 percent by 1966 and 22 percent by 1970.

THE TWO BASIC PROPOSALS

The proposal (1) to expand private consumer spending by wage rate increases, and the proposal (2) to increase Federal outlays on the ground (among others) that this is needed to

redirect demand toward areas where increases in private demand are not likely to add nearly enough to employment expansion, are entirely consistent.

Even in those areas where increases in private demand will
not add very greatly to employment expansion because of the
rate of advancing technology and automation, these increases
in private demand will nonetheless help to reverse the down-
ward trend in employment occurring in many of these areas,
and indeed promote some sizable increases. Further, the wage
increases will purchase goods and services which enter into improved living standards quite as much as public services. In
advocating enlargement of the "public sector," we should not
go overboard and lose perspective of the essential nature of our
economy, or of the prevalence of the private low living standards in our midst which are quite as shocking in human terms
and quite as inimical to economic growth and full employment
as the poverty in the public sector. Large advances are needed
on both the private and the public front.

Moreover, these two advances reinforce one another. Better
education and health services, when publicly financed, help
people to become fitted for higher grades of private employment. Higher grades of private employment, and higher wages
for productivity in the same employment, help people to pay
the cost of improved education and health services, either in
the form of private outlays or in the form of their contributions
to tax revenues. In short, the reduction of poverty and deprivation and the lifting of living standards in the United States are
one and the same problem as the problem of speeding up economic growth and achieving and maintaining maximum employment and production. A sufficiently comprehensive and
effective listing of the programs required for either of these

two purposes would turn out to be practically the same as a listing of the programs required for the other.[1]

[1] At the end of 1965, despite some reduction in unemployment and some acceleration of economic growth, I can find no reason to modify substantially the main points which I developed above in September, 1964. The rate of full-time unemployment as customarily measured is still at least 60 percent higher than it ought to be; instead of saying that this full-time unemployment is now at the lowest rate in eight years, we should be saying that never once within the past eight years have we come within hailing distance of the maximum employment to which we pledged ourselves as a nation under the Employment Act of 1946.

Taking into account the full-time equivalent of part-time unemployment and the concealed unemployment which results from scarcity of job opportunity, the true level of unemployment now is somewhere between 7 and 8 percent. Unemployment among young people and Negroes has not been very substantially reduced, and its concentration in these areas multiplies many times the extreme seriousness of the problem.

The rate of economic growth during the most recent years, despite the high claims made for it, has been very inadequate, for the only meaningful test of adequate economic growth, both quantitative and qualitative, is the rate required to reduce unemployment to minimum levels. Most of the recent deviations from what I regard to be efficient and equitable national economic policies remain about the same as they were as of September, 1964, with some further aggravation. During the most recent year, fostered by these economic policies, the rate of investment in the plant and equipment which add to our productive capabilities has been rushing forward several times as fast as the rate of increase in ultimate demand represented both by private consumption and public outlays. In terms of the great priorities of our national needs— for the rebuilding of our cities and the liquidation of the slums in which a fifth of our people still live, for bringing adequate medical care to the 40 percent of our people who cannot obtain it at costs within their means despite Medicare, for lifting our educational facilities and personnel to needed levels, for clearing our polluted water and air, for improving our mass transportation, and for conserving and replenishing our natural resources—we are still failing grossly to reallocate our resources. With changes only in minor detailing, I still stand for the policies and programs which I recommended in September, 1964.

LESSONS OF THE CLARK COMMITTEE MANPOWER HEARINGS

by Joseph S. Clark

Joseph S. Clark, U.S. Senator from Pennsylvania since 1957, served the city of Philadelphia as Controller and as Mayor from 1949 to 1956. He was in the USAAF in World War II and was a colonel at the time of his discharge. A member of the Board of Overseers of Harvard from 1953 to 1959, he received the Bok award in Philadelphia in 1956.

IN MAY, 1964 the Senate Subcommittee on Employment and Manpower, which I chair, issued its report titled "Toward Full Employment" and concluded that the nation is experiencing a "Manpower Revolution." By this we meant that technological innovation is having a profound impact upon the kind of labor force we need to staff the free American economy.

For most of the time since man came down out of the tree, began to utilize fire and invented the wheel, the manual labor of many has supported the leisure of a few. Toward the end of the eighteenth century the Industrial Revolution began the trend, which still continues, of drawing workers off rural farms and into urban factories.

But, as all of us know, during the early stages of industrial society the manual labor of the many continued to redound to the benefit of a privileged minority. There was little, if any, improvement of the lot of the manual worker in Europe. Only in America, where land was fertile and cheap, did a farm population arise which was partially independent—politically, socially, and economically.

Then, somewhat over a half century ago, something quite

new began to happen. In the more highly industrialized countries, particularly our own, the industrial and service base became highly developed—enough to start pouring forth abundance that had to be sold to and consumed by the many if the economy was to be sustained at a new and higher level. The "belt tightening" of early industrialization was at an end. In its place was a "mass consumption" society. From that point on, the consumer became a central figure in the economy. Our society began to require a continuing, moving cycle of mass consumption to sustain itself. Whenever the means of consumers were inadequate to purchase the goods needed to keep the cycle going fast enough, recession set in and the economy operated at but a fraction of its potential, with idle hands and idle plants.

This is one aspect of the "Manpower Revolution." It is a fact to which all too many Americans still remain oblivious, despite the clear demonstration of its validity shown by the impact of the recent tax cut. Simply stated, our free economy grinds to a halt in the absence of massive consumer purchasing power; and jobs for nearly all those willing to work are necessary to provide that purchasing power.

The later stages of industrialization have done more than create potential abundance for the masses of men. They have also altered, still more profoundly, the kind of work most of us do. The pick-and-shovel job is disappearing. The number of manual labor jobs is steadily shrinking relative to jobs in other sectors of the economy. More and more of a premium is placed on intellectual and technical skills. The service job is replacing the production job as the principal source of employment. This combination of potential affluence for all reasonably able workers and the upgrading of employable skills caused the "Manpower Revolution."

Inevitably, when any such deep change occurs in the nature of the manpower requirements of an economy, there are a number of transitional pains to which many find it difficult to accommodate.

This is particularly true right now.

For example, there are older people who, equipped with inadequate or obsolescent skills, find themselves too far down the road of life to go through that painful process of retraining and education which has suddenly become necessary if they are to find gainful employment again.

And there are those in the early years of middle age who, while perfectly capable of undertaking training for a new occupation, find it impossible to get at the required retraining, to find a job opening, or even to move perhaps thousands of miles to where the new job is located.

All too many of our youth are also up against it. Our labor force is expanding at an astounding rate, primarily because of the influx of millions of young people from the "war babies" generation. They have entered upon their lives as potential breadwinners without adequate training in an economy realizing considerably less than its job-employing potential. Jobs are in short supply for the untrained youth. Hundreds of thousands of them have found it impossible to get employment.

Nearly 9 million young workers have entered the labor force since 1960. Another 17 million will seek their first jobs in the next six years. This rate will continue until at least 1980. Unemployment among these young people has been between 2½ to 3 times the unemployment rate among adults. If they happen to be Negro, it is still higher.

In many cases the unemployed youth comes from an underprivileged environment in which ambition and motivation have been dangerously corroded by the hopelessness he sees around him. Of the more than 900,000 presently unemployed out-of-school youths between fourteen and twenty-four years of age, nearly half never graduated from high school. They left school because the world of work for which their education was supposed to train them was one which they did not feel qualified to join. The horizons of the slum hemmed in their aspirations. They are falling into idleness, despair, and, in all too many cases, delinquency.

It is the employment problem of these young people in which your committee is primarily interested.

How do we solve it? How do we eliminate this tragic social waste of America's young men and women? How do we produce the kind of labor force required to run the American economy of the future? These are some of the questions which our Senate Subcommittee on Employment and Manpower asked itself last year. They are the same questions you are asking yourselves today. I do not think either of us pretends that there is an easy answer, but I think we can agree that the solutions require action in several fields of public and private policy.

They lie first in our recognition that this new economy we have spawned must operate at levels of full efficiency if we are to preserve ourselves from the tragedies created by idle manpower. We must match trained, idle hands with idle machines and job openings in service industries.

We are no longer a nation of farmers, when an idle family always found enough to do, even during times of recession, just feeding and clothing itself.

In the mass-consumption, industrialized society of today, practically no one feeds and clothes himself. Industrial man must work for wages or salary to acquire the purchasing power to feed, clothe, and shelter himself.

We no longer live in the unregulated free economy described by Adam Smith. From day to day government and private industrial policies affect levels of production, employment, and purchasing power. This we agreed on when the Congress passed the Employment Act of 1946.

Accordingly, it behooves us to find and implement monetary, fiscal, employment and other policies which will result in maximum production, maximum employment, and reasonable price stability. This means properly using public taxing, expenditure, and monetary policies as a balance wheel or governor on the economy. As idle capacity and manpower rear their heads, tools used by the Federal government and private industry working together are used to put them back to work. As inflationary pressures build up, policies are invoked which temporarily deflate the economy to bring prices back in line. The Federal Budget can no longer be viewed as simply a fiscal document. It is an economic document as important as the report of the Council of Economic Advisers, and it should be so employed.

In my judgment, we are approaching a political-economic breakthrough in American life. Legislation based on the findings of our Subcommittee, to achieve a closer coordination between our Federal Budget policies and the state of our economy, is, it seems to me, an important requirement in raising our economy to full efficiency and full employment. But economic policy unrelated to manpower policy is meaningless if we are to attain full employment under modern conditions. Just as we try to find enough jobs for all those willing and able to work, we must also assure that our pool of adequately trained labor fits the needs of a highly sophisticated economy.

This will mean that we not only need to know how to educate a youngster for a world of work radically different from the one which existed when he enters first grade. It will also mean some reasonably sound prognosis on our part concerning the kind of world which lies ahead. In other words, comprehensive manpower planning.

We have come to the day when, as part of our war on poverty, we must embark upon very specialized educational efforts in our slums and deprived rural areas. We will have to provide a vehicle, such as a special nursery school program beginning at age three, which would afford the child an opportunity to spend a good part of each day in an environment in which he can be tutored and his ambitions fostered. All too often, raised in a slum home with no father under conditions of extreme deprivation, the child's aspirations, much less his ability to assimilate learning, have been destroyed by the time he reaches first grade.

But rescuing the child while still an infant will not be enough. We are going to have to find a way to bring the school experience more in line with the world in which the student will dwell. In the case of those who cannot or will not continue their schooling beyond high school, we must find a way of providing greater relevance between what he learns in the classroom and what he will know in the world of work. To those who can aspire to something more than a high-school education if only given a chance, we must provide at least fourteen years of free public education. That education must be attuned to the radically changing human condition.

It is important to separate, in concept at least, education from training for specific skills or occupations. The primary responsibility of the educational system is to teach people to think, not to prepare them for employment. Nevertheless, although the development of manpower resources is a secondary goal of education, the role of education is fundamental to full employment in an increasingly complex technological society. The goal of education should be to develop within each individual the ability to think logically and plan rationally, to understand himself in relationship to his enviroment, and to accumulate those basic intellectual tools necessary to a productive and meaningful life.

For many of the unskilled tasks of another generation which required primarily physical strength or manual dexterity, education was largely irrelevant to job-seeking. These tasks, however, have been the ones most susceptible to mechanization. Machines have been replacing the physical efforts of the human being for centuries, but at an accelerating pace in recent decades. Many simple, repetitive mental tasks requiring comparatively little education are now shifting into the realm of the computer. Man's superiority over the machine lies in his imagination, his rationality, and his emotional sensitivity, all in part products of education.

In practice, separation of education from training is difficult. The basic intellectual tools provided by formal education have become the prerequisites of successful training. Many have direct employment application. At the elementary and high-school level, however, the general principle is clear. The time has arrived in our complex world when the elementary and high schools have all they can do to inculcate in the student rationality, creativity, and the fundamental skills and knowledge necessary for communication and computation. A sound basic high-school education for everyone capable of assimilating it should be a minimal goal. Some courses of general value also have direct employment application—typing, for example.

Training for specific occupations should be post-secondary to the extent feasible, through higher vocational or technical education, through apprenticeship, and through on-the-job training. In recognition of the need for specialized training beyond high school, free public education should soon include at least vocational schools, technical schools, and junior or community colleges, so that up to fourteen years of education and training is available at public expense.

This does not deny the present contribution of and need for secondary-school level occupational training. Environmental deficiencies, our failure to provide an adequate educational system, particularly in economically and culturally deprived areas and neighborhoods, and the postwar flood of youth into the population have left us with a frightening backlog for whom the opportunity for a broader education is lost and employable skills an immediate need. But, as a long-run goal, it would be a serious mistake to concentrate educational resources upon specialized occupational preparation at the high-school level. Neither is there any implication that vocational or occupational training is of less value than general education, nor the occupations for which such training is provided less desirable than those dependent upon scholastic education. The argument is that occupational training should be added to, rather than in lieu of, at least the amount of general education which requires the full high-school years, even under the best of circumstances.

As a long-run goal, therefore, only those who are not able to profit from a general high-school curriculum because of environmental deficiencies or past failures of the educational system, should receive substantial occupational training at the secondary level. At the same time, the educational system should be flexible enough to provide for these people combination vocational-academic courses or work-study programs which can furnish as much intellectual preparation as possible while also supplying a salable skill.

At the other end of the educational spectrum, we must broaden the availability of higher education. Studies of the Office of Education have shown that 30 percent of the high-school seniors in the 80 to 90 percentile of their class and 43 percent of those in the 70 to 80 percentile fail to enter college. Approximately 40 percent of those who begin college withdraw before graduation. The nation is thus losing, through leakage in the educational system, a substantial portion of its brains and leadership potential.

For some the obstacle is motivation, but we are far from the point where higher education is equally available to all. The average direct cost of attending college is approximately $1,480 a year in public institutions and $2,240 a year in private institutions, an extremely large outlay from the current median family income of $5,700. As an illustration of the financial restraint, a study of 1960 high-school graduates found that only 13 percent of those who came from families with annual incomes under $4,000 went on to college, while 47 percent of those from families with annual incomes above $7,500 did so.

A mixture of motivational and financial factors is evident from the same study. It showed that 77 percent of the children of white-collar workers who had been in the top half of their high-school class went on to college, as did 45 percent of those from the lower half of their high school class. For children from non–white-collar workers who had been in the top half of their high-school class the percentage was 42, and from the lower half of the high school class, 18. Almost 12 percent of young white adults have completed college, but only 5.4 percent of nonwhites have done so. While 11 percent of the population is Negro, Negroes make up only 3.5 percent of all professional workers. Even though motivational factors, including those resulting from family background, were no doubt involved in many of these cases, financial abilities both in this generation and the last play a large role in determining who can and who cannot have the benefit of a college education. The loan provisions of the National Defense Education Act have been a boon to both the economy and individual students in making a college education available to those who might otherwise have been denied it. However, its funds have not been adequate to the demand. Scholarship funds also meet only a small fraction of the need.

The Senate Subcommittee on Employment and Manpower became convinced of the need for more personal financial assistance for students pursuing higher education. It has recommended a combination of programs affording scholarships, loans, and work-study assistance. This recommendation has been influential in the education bills considered by the Houses. In addition, the Committee supports the construction of community colleges throughout the nation, where two years of education beyond high school may be provided at public expense. But education in the classroom is not enough. Much of the training which a youth receives for the world of work will have to be on the job.

Let us take apprenticeship, for example. It is symptomatic of our failure to adequately train our youth.

In Great Britain between 35 and 40 percent of the boys enter formal apprenticeship programs upon completion of secondary school. In Germany, about 700,000 boys and girls leave school each year and about 420,000 of them enter some form of occupational training after graduation. In France, in 1959, there were 990,000 young men under twenty in the labor force, of whom about 450,000 were receiving vocational training.

By contrast, the United States, with 6 million fourteen to nineteen year olds and nearly 9 million twenty to twenty-four year olds has only a little over 200,000 apprentices and 2 million persons in vocational schools.

Apprenticeship and on-the-job training have a number of advantages which we are failing to exploit. The trainee is provided income and employment as well as experience and training. Training opportunities are tied directly to the demand for labor in the occupation. The training and work discipline acquired under apprenticeship cannot be duplicated in a vocational institution. Substantial public investment in plant and equipment is avoided because they are already available from the employer. Skilled craftsmen double as workmen and instructors.

But despite all these advantages, apprenticeships in the United States provide only a minor proportion of our requirements for skilled workers in any occupation.

Obviously, however, education and training for the future world of work will not make sense unless we can anticipate the kind of world into which we are moving. At the present time only a few experts have hazarded a guess about the occupational structure of the labor force which will exist when today's first-grader graduates from high school twelve years from now. I believe we must acquire the capacity to provide more enlightened guesses about the occupational structure today, five years from now, and a dozen years hence.

Using modern information technology, and a national network of job information and placement, we can conquer our ignorance in this key field.

One of the greatest hindrances to bringing together employers seeking workmen and employees seeking work is the relative lack of job-market information. If a labor market is to operate adequately, employers must know where to find the skills they need to do the job, and workers must know where the job opportunities lie. The present Federal-State Employment Service system is inadequate to this task. Employers rarely resort to it, except for the most menial kind of labor. Employees find job information restricted to a relatively small area in a very few occupations. Yet we have the technology and the system to provide a free interchange of information between employers and employees. The first step is to extend the area of job information to regional and national levels, connecting all employment offices into one giant job-information network.

The second step is to encourage more employers to list their job openings with the state employment services. This might be accomplished by providing a reduction in unemployment compensation tax to those employers willing to list their job openings with the state employment offices. Once a worker can depend on finding reasonably complete job information at his local employment office, he will be far less reluctant to go looking for work.

And finally, once our job-information network is operating at reasonably satisfactory levels, we will have a much clearer idea of the shifts in occupational structure in the American economy and be able to make far more intelligent guesses about what the future holds in store.

These are some of the things—expansionary economic policy, an education system addressed to future needs, and a national job-information network—which I feel are essential if we are to bring full employment to the United States and eliminate the tragic waste of idle employment.

CREATING MORE JOBS FOR YOUTH: AN ANTIUTOPIAN VIEW

by Ben B. Seligman

Ben B. Seligman is Professor of Economics and Director of the Labor Relations and Research Center of the University of Massachusetts. His publications include *Main Currents in Modern Economics, Poverty as a Public Issue,* and *Most Notorious Victory: Man in an Age of Automation.*

IT IS NOW commonplace to assert that the technology of our times will impose new burdens and new tasks on us all. We are told that in addition to requiring scientists, engineers, programmers, clerks, and salespeople to keep the cornucopia of the future flowing in prodigious quantities, we shall have to find ways of filling the empty time that will have been created. And it is said there will be no great problem, for people will learn to write poetry and play the oboe as they sit on the banks of the Wabash trying to catch the biggest fish in the river.

However, the utopia of the future beckons to us from a distant horizon, and it is only those blessed with hyperopia who are fortunate enough to discern its outlines. In the meantime, we who live in the present, while not perhaps antiutopian, must nevertheless wrestle with those situations that are apparent on a shorter time scale. And it is within that time scale that one must delineate the future shape of the work force, the increased capacity of American industry to produce, the patent incapacity of our society to distribute its industrial usufruct equitably, and the clear-cut indications that a large part of the populace will be endowed, or cursed, with a putative leisure not of their own making.

For the fact is that our economy is changing in ways that suggest a far lesser need for workers than has been the case in the past. The old pyramid, in which a large base of employed supported a narrower apex of nonworkers, is revolving about its center, so that soon, perhaps in a decade or two, a relatively few will provide the material requirements of the many. At the same time, these few may very well be "working" more hours than we should think conscionable. But that is another question, to which we need not address ourselves at the moment. In any case, to prepare for that contingency—the reversal of the work pyramid, which incidentally would indeed make automation meaningful—we should start now to reduce the work force. Of course, retraining is necessary to make square pegs round enough to fit into their proper holes. But in addition, a wage system that functioned well enough and at high enough levels to obviate, for example, the need for moonlighting and multiple-jobholders, would contribute enormously toward alleviating the strains of automation. A variegated works program, geared to rebuilding the neglected "social overhead" in the public realm—roads, parking space, school buildings, urban transport, housing, and parks—would not only give jobs to several million of the untutored, but also, over the long haul, provide them with minimal work skills. And for those unlikely ever to work again, of which there must be at least a million or more (aside from the aged), why not simply give them enough money to carry on with some measure of decency?

But as we dream these dreams, the centuries-old habits of American politics intrude. An archaic ethic which insists that he who does not work shall not eat; a Congressional structure virtually unchanged since colonial days; a federalism that fails to come to grips with the complexities of regional economies; an apathetic response from the affluent; and the American posture of make-do and sudden crash programs—all these raise seemingly insuperable barriers to the formulation of a reasonable program to deal with automation and new technology and its consequences.

Let us see what the prospects are for the work force in the age of burgeoning automation, or if you prefer, cybernation. I can only sketch the prospects in most general terms here. It has been argued by some that modern technology will require a shift to occupations demanding more education and higher skills. This may be so—but only up to a point. For the indications are that such a process, known as upgrading, cannot continue without abatement. As Professor James R. Bright has so well demonstrated, at some point there no longer is a need for more technicians and more programmers.[1] Once the computer has been given its assignments, once all the programs and instructions have been stored in its memory to calculate payrolls, accounts receivables, inventory, personnel records, depreciation charges, and the like, it will require little further attention. Moreover, once an automatic factory has been "debugged" so that it will meekly obey the instructions of its computer master, there is but a minimum need for maintenance. Thus, if we examine the situation with a sober, not a starry-eyed, glance, we shall discover that the high priests of the automated society have been voicing pieties rather than realities.

The consequence, it seems to me, is that we shall continue to contend with persistent unemployment. The situation today, despite our affluence, is indeed perturbing. One may hazard

[1] J. R. Bright, "Some Effects of Automation upon Wage Determination," in G. Friedrichs, ed., *Automation und Technischer Fortshritt in Deutschland und den USA* (Frankfurt, 1963), p. 139.

the guess that at least a fifth of our officially unemployed today can attribute their condition to technological displacement. Seasonal factors and new entrants probably account for another two-fifths; frictional movements for perhaps a tenth; and lagging effective demand may be the cause of the remaining three-tenths. However, if we add to the government's count about 1½ million of the invisible unemployed—those too discouraged even to hunt for jobs—and perhaps 500,000 or so full-time "equivalents" for those working part time, not because they want to but because that is all they can obtain, then "real" unemployment, as Leon Keyserling so rightly calls it, begins to approach 9 percent of the work force, and structural unemployment begins to approach half the total.

One may very well ask how these estimates may be reconciled with the fact that the number of jobs did grow from 1953 to 1963. The point is that job expansion took place primarily in government and government procurement programs and in nonprofit agencies. Private industry run for profit simply failed to provide any jobs at all. In fact, it can be shown that there was in all probability a drop in full-time employment in that sector. During the 1953–63 decade, the civilian labor force increased by 8.9 million; employment gained 6.6 million; however, unemployment also increased—by 2.3 million. The net increase of full-time jobs was 2.5 million, and in part-time jobs, 3.2 million. If we distribute the 900,000 persons on vacation and other leaves in the same proportions, we obtain gains in full-time workers during the decade of 3.1 million and of part-time workers of 3.5 million. The increase in government employment was 2.8 million, all of it virtually full-time. The total nongovernment gain was about 500,000; but nonprofit agencies provided an additional 1½ million jobs in the ten years. Hence, if but half of the latter was but full-time, it would absorb the

500,000 nongovernmental gain and thereby indicate a decline in full-time employment offered by private business.[2]

Shall we, then, send all new entrants into the labor force and all those displaced by machines to work for that great under-writer, the government? And here I mean government at all levels—Federal, state, and local. This is most unlikely, considering the structure of government employment. In 1962, of 9.2 million government workers, almost a third were professional and technical persons, half of them teachers. Clerical and skilled craftsmen comprised almost another third, leaving some 3 million jobs in the service, unskilled, and other categories. What prospect, then, is there for government employment for the 1½ million new entrants into the labor force each year, or for the million or million and a half persons who will be displaced by technology in the next decade?

I fear there will be little consolation for the factory worker in the expansion of government employment (which has resulted primarily from the assumption of more tasks), since he does not possess the requisite transferable skills. In any event, according to a recent joint report by the departments of Labor and Commerce, further growth in the number of Federal jobs seems doubtful. To make matters worse, employment is also expected to drop because of technology in eighteen major in-

[2] Note, Nov. 1965: Over the long run this analysis is not to be depreciated because jobs have increased substantially in 1964–65, or because the unemployment rate is down so sharply. Let us observe that while the tax cut in 1964 did increase gross national product by $27 billion, unemployment dropped by not quite 400,000: the rate itself declined about $2/10$ of one percent. It was not until other Federal programs, such as the Neighborhood Youth Corps, plus the war in Vietnam, had exerted their full economic force that the unemployment figures dropped precipitately—a 400,000 decline in the *first three quarters of 1965*, or $3/5$ of one percent; that is, down to 4.4 percent of the work force. Employment itself rose simply because the new activity brought more people who had left the work force back to jobs. That "solutions" must be achieved by measures external to the normal functioning of the economy suggests a certain irony.

dustries which have up to now enjoyed high volume—automobiles, iron and steel, electric power, and the like. In fourteen other industries, moreover—including trade, banking, insurance, transport, electronics, and synthetics—only increased demand can apparently overcome the effects of spreading labor-saving devices.

The fundamental economic relationships involved are very simple: As productivity (i.e., the power to produce) increases, there must be a concomitant increase in output, or jobs are bound to disappear. Technology, in part a child of the state, has given a fillip to productivity, but production has not been increasing fast enough to provide all the jobs we need for an ever growing population. Here are the facts: from 1909 to 1947, the average annual increase in productivity was 2 percent; from 1947 to 1960, it was about 3 percent; and from 1960 to 1963, it rose 3.6 percent each year. With such an annual rise in productivity, and with 60 million people in the private labor force, 2.1 million new jobs would have to be created every year just to keep unemployment from going up, and another 1.5 million a year would be needed to take care of the young people just coming into the work force. Now, while output has indeed been on the increase, the pace of the increase has been too sluggish to compensate for the enhanced productivity stemming from automation, mechanization, cybernation; that is, from the new technology.

The answer, then, would appear to be simple: Just increase output. That, however, is more easily said than done, for there is no way of bringing about greater output (at least in the private sector) when there are no jobs. One possible solution—which is indeed on the verge of adoption by default—is to allow Disraeli's "two nations" to develop once again and let the poor go hang. Another solution—advanced by those who believe that fiscal policy alone can cure the affliction of unemployment no matter what its etiology may be—is to create additional output by such means as the 1964 tax cut, which is expected to generate an additional thirty billion dollars' worth of demand. But the real likelihood is that even an expanded demand of this magnitude could not do much for foot-loose miners, unemployed packinghouse workers, displaced auto workers, laid-off railroad workers, and all the others whose skills have suddenly become unnecessary and unwanted. To be sure, the Council of Economic Advisers argued before the Senate Labor Committee in 1963 that there is a "proven capacity for a free labor market to reconcile discrepancies between particular labor supplies and particular labor demand." [3] Yet in recent years the gross national product has grown as much as 6 percent per annum, and no new jobs have come into being for those who need them most bitterly—the displaced, the young, the unskilled. The industries in which displacements have been occurring are mature ones—automobiles, steel, food-processing, clothing—and it seems highly improbable that they will expand their sales sufficiently to replace the jobs that have been dispensed with. Automation has accelerated productivity in these industries just enough for them to keep pace with normal market growth while getting along with fewer workers.

What, then, are we to do? There are some who say that precedent for government action was provided by the Full Employment Act of 1946. But this statute does not even offer a rough blueprint. Failing to define what "full employment" goals ought to be in an economy that undergoes perpetual change, the Act, which directs the Council of Economic Advisers merely to study conditions and write reports, remains what it was intended to be—a superb example of legislative rhetoric.

[3] Statement to Senate Committee on Labor and Welfare, September, 1963.

If one looks at the debates in Congress preceding its passage, one finds much talk on fiscal and monetary policy and how the Federal Reserve System might stimulate investment by manipulating interest rates and member bank reserves and by buying and selling securities in the open market. Unfortunately, the Federal Reserve System is still a quasi-independent agency, and it has not always pursued policies that would benefit the rest of us. The Full Employment Act, therefore, is of little help in an age of automation.

The pressures on government to do something, however, continued, and they finally did boil over in 1961 into the first major piece of legislation to deal with structural unemployment—the ARA, which authorized the spending of $375 million to stimulate economic activity in depressed areas. Most of the money was earmarked for long-term loans, and some of it for grants to local communities. Since the measure was not intended to deal specifically with the aftermath of automation, only a modest sum was allocated for teaching the unemployed new skills.

By the end of 1963, over $200 million had been committed, presumably enough to create 20,000 new jobs in areas long afflicted by joblessness. Additional funds were refused in the summer of 1964, however, and the ARA may be doomed to expire in futility.

One thing the ARA experience revealed was the urgent need for a viable manpower policy. It is a need that arises not only from the high unemployment rates which persist despite prosperity, and from the monthly influx of thousands of teenagers into the labor market, but from the dislocations created by automation as well. Of course, the employment situation is complicated; disentangling in statistically precise ways the variety of elements involved is almost impossible. We can at best engage in intelligent guessing. While some unemployment may be attributed to lagging effective demand, computer technology and rapid obsolescence of older methods of making goods have destroyed numerous skills while creating other more esoteric occupations which themselves require fewer bodies to fill. Hence, no amount of heat emanating from a warmed-up fiscal policy will melt the icebergs of hard-core unemployment. Existing measures such as the tax cut are like trying to light a match to Antarctica. But what of the other measures that have been adopted—vocational education, retraining, and programs to improve labor mobility? How have they been faring?

Let us consider retraining. Essential as they are, training programs are not a solution to unemployment. As one economist has remarked, they are rather a salvaging operation to help a few individuals acquire marketable skills. The fact remains that most of the unemployed could not fill the jobs for which there may be openings even if they got a whole decade's training. Most of those in charge of the training programs acknowledge this, and motivated by an understandable bureaucratic desire for success, they have had to impose high admission standards, select the courses carefully, and concentrate on younger people. Consequently, older persons and women have by and large been overlooked. (While 10 percent of all Manpower Development and Training Act programs involve persons over the age of forty-five, more than a quarter of the unemployed fall into this age bracket.)

How successful has the training effort been thus far? Labor Department officials say that 88 percent of those who completed their courses got jobs. This sounds impressive until one translates it back into the actual numbers: in 1963 only 27,500 unemployed persons (out of a total of 65,000 who originally enrolled) received training, and of these only 17,000 were able to put it to use successfully. Obviously, much more needs to be done if training is to have any sort of impact. Officials may believe that they have an unqualified success on their hands, but 27,500 graduates a year will not meet Congress's hope for 400,000 retrained workers within three years. At best, it is but a useful start.

It may very well be that the ultimate long-run solution is to create a smaller active work force, or as Robert Heilbroner has put it, to shift the supply curve for labor to the left.[4] This is precisely what has been happening ever since the National Origins Act cut off our foreign labor supply in 1921. Social security further reduced the work force by telling people that they do not have to work up to the moment they drop dead. At the other end of the age spectrum, compulsory education laws have helped keep youngsters out of the work force. And the progressive shortening of the work-week over the last fifty years in a sense has represented a curtailment of the labor supply.

As might be expected, the latter suggestion always sets devotees of the conventional wisdom to shivering as they warn that a reduction in weekly hours from forty to thirty-five implies an intolerable labor cost increase of 14 percent. But such arithmetic stops short of the complete analysis, since labor cost as proportion of total cost or of revenue may be as low as 25 percent. Thus a 14 percent increase in the labor component may be but a 2 or 3 percent increase in comparison to revenue. Considering industry's incessant push for more and more sales and its great capacity to produce, such a modest jump in cost could be absorbed quite easily. Indeed, was this not the history

[4] Personal communication, March, 1964.

of hours-reduction over the last half century, when on the average the work-week has been reduced by fifteen minutes a year? Those who fear a burden of cost stemming from a shorter work-week must explain how it was possible to get down to forty hours or less today.

Ultimately, all of these problems come down to politics, not in the narrow sense of maneuvers and endorsements, but in the fundamental sense of planning and perspective. This can be a painful situation. Programs must be sold to legislators who all too frequently consider the Federalist papers and the speeches of Calhoun to be the touchstones of eternal wisdom. It is this problem—antecedent to all the proposed solutions for automation—to which we must face up if we are to escape the tyranny of the machine.

The displaced need to be shifted to jobs still available. (The printing trades unions in Washington recently claimed that there were several hundred openings for which people might be trained; government bureaucrats disbelieved the unions— consequently, no training program.) We ought to encourage secondary wage earners to stay home. (They will if the bread-winner earns enough.) People might be drawn into voluntary community activity. (*Vide* the fantastic response to the domestic peace corps idea.) Why not give longer vacations, sabbaticals, travel grants? (As Herbert Gans said in an article in *The Correspondent* in 1963, this might "professionalize" a good many occupations.) Perhaps the introduction of new equipment ought to be licensed. (Not to inhibit or eliminate them, but to apply them in accordance with a timetable that would avoid the present helter-skelter uses of technology.) Keep teen-agers in school. (But for heaven's sake let's improve the education system!) And finally, let us simply give money to those who have not enough and will never earn enough—the aged, indigent, and shattered. (It might sound better if this were referred to as more extensive transfer payments.)

All this needs to be done soon; otherwise, a vast trauma awaits us all.

GUIDELINES FOR IMPROVED
PUBLIC POLICY

by John H. Rubel

John H. Rubel is Director of the Fast Deployment Logistics Ship Project of Litton Industries, Inc. He was on loan from that company to the President's Task Force for the War on Poverty for three months in 1964, and continues as consultant to Sargent Shriver's Business Leaders' Advisory Council and in occasional special assignments. He is Chairman of the Scientific Advisory Board of the National Security Agency. In addition to participating in affairs of government and industry, he has lectured at the University of California and the University of Illinois and has written numerous articles and documents.

OUR CHIEF concern is not simply that unemployment is said to be high among teenagers and young adults. Our chief concern is that this teenage wave will move through our society for the next forty years, the leading edge of a massive and growing current of people who cannot or will not choose to play a role which either they or the rest of America considers up to American standards, a current increasingly separated in achievement, aspirations, and world view from the rest. It is because we see a mismatch between these people and the institutions in which they ought to find a place but probably won't that we see today's problem as tomorrow's crisis.

If we had old-fashioned confidence in the adaptability of the people we are talking about, this would seem much less of a public issue. If we thought that the mismatched institutions—factories, offices, schools, government bureaus, farms, ships—

all the places where people learn and work—could and would adjust themselves amply and swiftly to the needs of the unemployed youths who threaten to grow into unemployed adults and the fathers and mothers of still less employable and more numerous offspring, then too it would seem like much less of a public issue, or a matter of public policy. The trouble is that we can see diverging trends here that worsen the mismatch. The people, unaided or improperly aided, will find adjustments getting harder all the time. Institutions can increasingly dispense with the unadjusted people. Without changes, youth unemployment will worsen, not improve. It calls for public concern not just for the unemployed youths but for the society that includes them. It calls for public action because unaided private actions are not going to be adequate or timely. The very existence of the problem shows that.

Any discussion of public policies concerned with this problem will split along these two lines. Some policies will be aimed at people. If there is a mismatch between the capabilities of people and the requirements of institutions, it is logical and necessary to improve the match by changing and improving the people. Programs in education, job training, and even the bussing of children from poor districts to public schools in other parts of the same city can be grouped under this broad heading.

Some policies are aimed at institutions, although generally public policy has less scope for action and immediate effect in this domain. Can employers be induced to lower the educational requirements they have set up for jobs that ought to call for comparatively simple training and little by way of formal education? Can labor unions be induced to help find ways to admit willing and able youngsters to apprenticeship in trades increasingly closed to new entrants, which often practice racial discrimination to boot? Can schools be changed, or if not changed, supplemented by additional institutions where achievement, not rate of achievement, is the measure of success?

The two lines of policy, and their advocates, are often in conflict. At one extreme are those convinced of the perfection of our institutions. Any mismatch between people and institutions must be attributed to people. The simplistic attitude is to let them suffer for their deficiencies. The rationale says that suffering is an incentive to correct through self-help what otherwise will be indefinitely perpetuated and even amplified through outside assistance. Common sense—a concern for the social and political consequences of the problem of youth unemployment—acknowledges the need for programs of habilitation and rehabilitation, even at this end of the spectrum of social philosophy.

And at another extreme I suppose you will find would-be architects of a new social order better geared to the needs of those that haven't made it in this one. One begins convinced of the perfectibility of people. Their imperfections as economic and social men must be attributed to the society that conditioned them. Here the simplistic view holds that it is up to society to change itself so that it will induce further changes in people in directions needed by society and wanted by those advocates of change who can perceive what is good for both society and the people in it.

Hopefully this discussion will not focus on such differences. Hopefully it will be possible to concentrate on facts to the extent they are known and a balanced assessment of the impact of a family of policies, rather than advocacy of this one or that. I am an engineer by training. Engineering problems are not solved in conference. Successful solutions do not come out of advocacy for this approach or that piece of gadgetry. I would hope that our approach here, and the approach to the formulation of public policies, could be governed by a corresponding objectivity.

The analogy has relevance, I think. Youths are unemployed for many reasons. Their need to be employed varies greatly. Their employability is very much a function of their capacities, motivations, intelligence, skills, attitudes—but also of the general economic climate in the country, barriers to employment that have nothing to do with competence or will, swift changes in the conditions and nature of work, and the environmental factors that affect all these and more. The task must be tackled by addressing all such factors in concert. We should not stint in our efforts to understand every term in the complex social equation that describes the problem. Any discussions we have or policies that are formulated ought to begin from this perspective.

In fact, this is really my first guideline: Constantly seek ways to formulate new policies and programs in a framework that accounts for their mutual interaction. Define the "problem" broadly enough so that the relevance of interrelated policies and programs will be clear to the architects of each as well as to the architects of the whole. I will return to this notion later on.

It is difficult for me to be precise about the problem we would like to discuss. We are not really concerned about the unemployment of all the youths that are classified as unemployed. Conversely, we may be concerned about the actual employment of a number who are not so counted. Briefly, we are not concerned in this discussion with the feebleminded, the sick, the criminally insane, kids looking for part-time work so they can buy a roadster, or teenage moonlighters looking for a second job. Obviously, also, attendance at school extending the period of preparation in anticipation of greater rewards later on is employment. We are concerned chiefly with youngsters who can't get a steady job of any kind, who can't earn enough to support a family and apparently never will, who know that they need to work and want to. And we are concerned with youths who have chosen idleness instead of work either because they were never motivated otherwise or because they are overwhelmed by discouragement.

The factors that bear on the problem as loosely defined here are pretty well agreed upon. Discrimination against colored and other minorities needs no restatement. The correlation of employment and income with education is so striking that one almost has to conclude that the opposite correlation applies, too—that the dropouts, push-outs, drift-outs, and rejectors of the public high school will be more often unemployed than the others. Some conclude that continuing them in high school to graduation should, ipso facto, improve their employability. Whether that follows is debatable. No doubt the factors that are making millions of teenagers into dropouts of one kind or another bear heavily on their prospects for employment whether they finally graduate from high school or not. Many of these factors—cultural deprivation in early years, inadequacies of slum schools, the compound amplification of social and intellectual handicaps among culturally disadvantaged people often crowded but increasingly isolated—are getting lots of attention precisely because their impact on long-range employability seems obvious.

And finally, there is the problem of the widening gap between the preparation that youths need to get and the preparation many are getting for full participation in economic and social life. I suspect this gap can be easily exaggerated. Automation and cybernation are not the apocalyptic malady they are sometimes portrayed to be. There is plenty of room for ordinary people with ordinary skills doing ordinary jobs with competence and a liberal dose of bourgeois virtues like thrift, diligence, workmanship, and pride. Still, the better jobs take increasingly better preparation. The young adult who is preparing to be an adult naturally suffers from an assortment of problems from identity crisis to adolescent sex. Those who haven't made it, those for whom the period of preparation has ended, and who cannot identify themselves with bright prospects at the end of their apprenticeship, are bound to seek new identities. Whatever the identity crisis of this individual or that may be, the threat of a growing separatist movement swelled by a growing crowd of unemployed teenagers who grow into adulthood still unemployed, followed by a swift current of still more teenagers like they were, could swiftly become a clear and present danger. Where would their attachments drift, no longer fixed to the American dream? So it is mandatory to find ways to reach to the heart of this confrontation.

One means is through extending the period of youthful preparation in a new way, through new mechanisms, in a new context, in the hope of rescuing at least some of those youths who would otherwise be—and see themselves as—increasingly adrift from the mainstream of economic opportunity and social participation. The new Job Corps created under the Economic Opportunity Act of 1964 is a leading example of such a mechanism.

It is important, too, to find ways to reach youths where they are, and work with them in an effort to bridge the self-image, self-perception gap. In a greatly oversimplified sense one can see this as a problem in management. We have it in every large organization. The ordinary tasks are discharged by those of ordinary capacities. Management handles the complex decisions and emergencies. The competence of managers amplifies the usefulness of others.

A similar principle applies to reaching the youngster whose period of active preparation for the future has ended and whose prospects for success are dim. Without management he is likely to succumb to the divisive and unwanted influences that are surrogates for economically and socially useful participation in the greater society. With it he may be able to get along reasonably well. Big Brother movements have operated on this premise with great success. Public policies that encourage the development and extension of such activities are in the right direction. In fact, they are really essential, not as substitutes for the initiative of local groups but as catalysts that will encourage their formation and support their expansion. Perhaps no single factor will prove more important in dealing with youths now unemployed than this creation of policies and programs that will reach the boys and girls who are adrift and try to orient them through guidance, counsel, and personal sponsorship.

Let us return to the guidelines I spelled out in the opening pages. I urged there that the "problem" of youth unemployment be defined broadly enough so that the relevance of interrelated policies and programs will be clear to the architects of each and to the architects of the whole. By the architecture of the whole I have in mind the application, over time, of as much as possible of the "project" approach to the interrelated problems that cluster around the problem of youth unemployment.

The Poverty Bill seems like a good start in this direction. It combines in a single legislative package the concepts and authorities that span a multitude of functions. Ordinarily those functions would have been separated out and handled individually by the responsible departments. As it is they are handled both distributively and centrally, with the Office of Economic Opportunity clearly assigned the manager's role. This could inaugurate a new look in both policy and action. If it does it can, I think, open up new opportunities all along the line. Now, with a project approach targeted on a set of objectives well specified in advance, the whole set of interrelated programs needed to reach those objectives can be set up with much greater freedom and many fewer impediments. The natural tendency of proponents of this program or that approach to act as if they held the single key to future success will be greatly diminished.

When you have a project responsible for a total end result, the relative role of each functional specialty, each functionally directed activity, is more easily adjusted to the needs to be met and levels of activity required to meet them. The orientation toward project goals, dictated by a desired end result, helps all around. The functional contributors, working together under project aegis, develop a unique sort of collective wisdom out of which new insights spring. Each functional contributor senses the goad and the constraints of project goals, and this introduces a wholesome tendency to polarize each subordinate undertaking in the direction of the wanted end result. It lessens competition and amplifies coordination. It creates a collective intelligence greater than the sum of the otherwise unlinked elements that make it up.

And if projects can be set up on a proper basis, the opportunity then arises to promote a new articulation of public purpose with private means. If, for example, Job Corps Urban Training Centers are run under contract to industrial firms, we may see ourselves moving down a new path in an unexplored direction. There, in that direction, lies a new articulation, a new way of connecting the private and the public sector. We have created such an articulation in space and defense. It is here that vast projects have blazed the trail for project organizations and the techniques of systems analysis so much wondered at these days. Here, on space and military projects, the private industrial sector has assumed a changed character, purposefully modified to meet the needs of new markets, existing in a unique symbiosis with the agencies for space and defense. Projects in the socioeconomic domain could lead to analogous developments. They would create new markets and lead to new relationships between the public and private sectors. They would alter the traditional role of the private sector in relation to public programs and policies. The private sector would be given an enlarged role and a bigger stake in the design and execution of public efforts that are intended to impinge directly upon the development not of missiles or satellites, but of major segments of our own society.

Here, then, is a further extension of our starting guideline. It tells us that we should begin by defining the "problem" broadly enough so that the chief relevant policies and programs will be grouped under the problem heading so that they may be addressed in context. And it goes on to say that we should try to organize the attack on such "problems" by using the "project" approach wherever we can. That approach opens up the opportunity to orchestrate properly the talents and actions of functional specialists. It opens up further possibilities for a new articulation of public purpose with private means—the purposeful involvement of private firms, under contract, with major portions of the responsibilities held under project auspices.

I seek such a new articulation, because through it I see opening up a new involvement of private industry in programs serving basic public needs. Such an articulation would unleash talents, insights, and energies in the private sector that for the most part have never been directed specifically to socioeconomic concerns. If they are so unleashed, I would look for something of the renaissance in method and achievement in these fields that has marked our unprecedented advance in modern technology under the aegis of military and space projects. I would certainly expect to see the swift evolution of new perceptions, new attitudes, and growing support, as major elements of the private sector became involved in and identified with publicly supported socioeconomic programs.

The initial key, it seems to me, lies in the organization of the government for its attack on problems of youth unemployment, poverty, urban development, housing, and a host of related problems. The complex interrelationship of these problems is growing. The importance of tie-ins among them is better recognized all the time. Creating mechanisms within the government for managing those interconnections is the next big, important step. Perhaps the Office of Economic Opportunity will be the first of a series of new-style organizations that will combine the best talents of existing agencies with the streamlined power of the project system. Again, to use a far-fetched analogy, that is how we did it and do it in space and for the military. It is not necessary, and certainly not desirable, to reorganize established departments around each new project. But it is necessary to set up project organizations in a framework that can properly focus, harness, and direct the talents and capabilities needed for each major project. Then ad hoc organizations can mobilize the resources of functional agencies. The goals can be set up to focus the contributions of each. The private sector can be given major responsibilities under contract.

That is what I visualize as a new weapon in the assault on

problems like "youth unemployment." First, define the "problem" carefully. Prepare the "specifications," the goals to be accomplished. Then organize the project group with authority to meet the specifications. And seek, in the process, new ways to benefit from the interdisciplinary nature of the orchestrated team working toward project goals. Seek, too, ways to imitate the space and military example in finding new patterns for the growing and novel articulation of public purposes and private means. Specifically, create a market place for the contract services of the private business and industry sector that will assign major chunks of responsibility to it. That is the way to capture the imagination and secure the informed support of the private sector for engineering directed inward toward launching an ever greater society toward a brightening future. The specific task, the most important single task, is to begin now to think through steps for the implementation of the guidelines sketched in this paper.

NEEDED: A NEW PERSPECTIVE

by Eli Ginzberg

Eli Ginzberg, whose most recent publications are *Life Styles of Educated Women* and *Talent and Performance*, is Professor of Economics in the Graduate School of Business and Director of the Conservation of Human Resources Project at Columbia University. He is Chairman of President Johnson's National Manpower Advisory Committee and is consultant to five Cabinet Departments— State, Defense, Commerce, HEW, and Labor.

FIRST, let me set quickly before you some convictions about youth unemployment. Since the labor market always adjusts to the educational level of the population as a whole, there is little basis for the simplistic contention that jobs are going begging primarily because a lot of people are uneducated or untrained. Nor do I think it is possible to deal with youth unemployment as an isolated problem, without noting that youth is competing with all the other actual and potential members of the labor force. While there may be distinctive and special characteristics of unemployed young people, a sensible perspective on the issue can be had only within the larger framework of the entire unemployment problem.

A third conviction relates to the fact that the figures on unemployment gravely understate the number of people interested in and capable of working. It is impossible to codify those who want to work or are able to work unless they are actively seeking a job. Snatches of evidence indicate that the number of young people not in school and not at work have an unemployment rate three times as high as the calculated rate.

Next, there is currently under way a big program to attack adult illiteracy. While all types of remedial programs of this nature are highly desirable (and I take some pride in having written one of the first books about the uneducated), the first and more important job is to answer the needs in the lower school system. It is foolish and inefficient to invest money to remedy the failure of the schools, without putting money lower in the system to ensure that no child leave school without control over the basic skills of reading, writing, and simple calculation. It is certainly possible to achieve this minimum standard, except with children who are mentally or emotionally unable to learn. The reason we have so many adult illiterates is simply that the schools have been grossly deficient.

Now to some speculations based on these convictions. Some historical background helps focus our present problems. For instance, the United States used to keep its labor reserves in Europe, and now it has them at home. Europe used to carry our unemployment load; when we needed labor, we drew it from Europe. Second, we used to hide our labor reserves on the farms and now they are sitting in the cities.

Another change finds us entering a period with an unusual rate of increase in the number of young people and with more and more married women becoming attached to the labor force. In 1963 more women than men got jobs in the United States.

A fourth aspect relates to the long-term differences in the quality of education and other developmental experiences between rural and urban areas, and between South and North. These differences, increased by the great mobility of the American population, have resulted in a situation in the Northern and Western cities in which some people are one to two generations behind the norm in the quality of their preparation for

NEEDED: A NEW PERSPECTIVE

work. A youngster brought up on an Alabama or Mississippi farm who lands in Detroit, San Francisco, or New York, is two generations behind in his preparation for life. A tremendous part of the youth unemployment problem is a result of such migration.

Next, the Negro revolution currently under way is intermingled with, but is still to be distinguished from, unemployment in general and youth unemployment specifically. This revolution is very beneficial to certain Negroes who are in a position to take advantage of it, but it is doing relatively little for the many other Negroes who are not in a position to avail themselves of the opportunities in the changes in the economic, educational, and social systems. Sixty percent of the Negro population is still locked up in the South. The fact that the South historically has been the great manpower surplus area of the United States explains why total Negro figures look so poor: sixty percent of the Negroes are fighting for a position in the economy against whites who themselves have a hard time.

The sixth point is that we can distill out of all the confusing contentions about the nature of technological change and productivity a few very simple but unequivocal generalizations. One is that the machine is increasingly eliminating the jobs which require little or no skill. Although the rate at which jobs are being eliminated or created is not clear, it is clear that productivity is higher in terms of a ratio of input to output in recent years. Although we are not all going to be unemployed tomorrow, we are able to turn out more goods and services with fewer input factors than ever before.

Therefore, with the rapid elimination of semiskilled and unskilled jobs—the historic routes into work for young people— the only other major route into work is a substantial degree of educational background for a wholly different set of jobs. A strong back is no longer a guarantee for getting work, but a good head should find work, for the time being at least.

The next point is that we are dealing with human beings with their multiple problems. Already we see a vicious cycle operating within childhood and adolescence. A large portion of the unemployed youths come from poverty-stricken homes, grow up in communities with inadequate services, and often get into early trouble with the law. Census data indicate that young Negroes are institutionalized at a rate of about three times that of young whites. A period in the reformatory is poor preparation for adulthood, and former inmates have a particularly difficult time finding jobs. As a result of this vicious cycle, many youngsters reach adulthood without any hope.

My next speculation is complicated but important. Our newspapers, economists, and political leaders refer to three concepts that used to be identified but which may now have broken apart. One is the concept of the impressive general economic growth of the country. The second is that corporate profits are an important hallmark of a successful economy. Economic growth gives one dimension, corporate profits or, if you prefer, per capita income, give another. In addition, we have the concept of jobs and employment. Historically the country grew, business was prosperous, the real income of the population went up rapidly, and jobs were plentiful. All went together. Now, however, we are living through a period in which the country is growing quite rapidly, in which corporate profits are very good, in which per capita income is moving up very nicely. Nevertheless we have problems on the employment front. Our old concepts are no longer congruent with reality. This fact has implications completely for economic and general policy and particularly for policy having to do with youth employment.

I do not want to be accused of arguing that it would be possible for our economy to manifest—surely not over any considerable period of time—a growing gross national product, a high level of corporate profits, and mounting unemployment. But for shorter periods of time, divergences between the conventional criteria of economic growth and employment trends are possible and may be quite substantial.

We passed an Employment Act in 1946, but we have not been concerned with its implementation. This is not because Congress is made up of archconservatives; its performance in recent years indicates that it is not. But the Employment Act was a revolutionary doctrine for a basically conservative country. Consequently, even though Congress committed itself to a revolutionary doctrine, it did not know quite what to do with it. Being pragmatic, it moved slowly. Congress gave certain instructions to the President; it gave itself certain instructions about various policy actions; and there has been movement to adjust fiscal and budgetary policy to accomplish the goals of the Employment Act.

Then, with the passing of the ARA in 1961, and particularly with the MDTA in 1962, Congress took another step forward in an attempt to do something about the people who are being ejected from their conventional jobs with no further use for their conventional skills. It decided first to establish training programs and recently it has gone further in establishing the Economic Opportunity Act. But Congress is still restive about how fast or how far it ought to go to implement the central commitments of the Employment Act. There are, certainly, good reasons to be bothered, because, while it is possible for the Federal government to create jobs, everything the Federal government does has a cost as well as a benefit built into it. The question of how to move from, let us say, employment of 95 percent to employment of 97 percent of the potential employables is a complicated one which will involve much imagination and innovation if serious costs such as inflation are to be avoided.

That is the nub of the issue. It is always easier for the government to take action when there is a very large number of unemployed, such as during the Depression of the 1930s, because in a crisis it need not be concerned about the cost. But as we move toward a full-employment economy, the question is posed whether tinkering with the situation will give a net asset or net deficit. No instruments have been worked out either by academicians or by administrators by which we can know how to establish the needed additional two to three percent of employment. So Congress has been cautious.

Since youth unemployment depends upon how many other people want jobs, I have been interested in all kinds of action taken by Congress to help those people withdraw from the labor force who want to leave. I viewed with favor, therefore, the amendment to the Social Security Act whereby Congress reduced optional retirement to sixty-two. I would like to consider some further moves, such as the establishment of a new "permanently unemployable" category under the Social Security System for persons between fifty-eight and sixty-two of little education and skill who lose their jobs. A man should not be forced to use up all of his savings waiting to reach the age when he qualifies for Social Security. In any case, I would like to see as much experimentation at the upper end of the scale as possible, not to force anybody out of the labor force but to encourage them to withdraw.

Next, I have long held a position, in advance of this Administration and the preceding one, that while shortening the hours of work alone would not spectacularly ease the unemployment situation in the short run, it is necessary and desirable for long-

run balance. Since the beginning of the century we have taken
out 40 percent of our increasing productivity in reduced hours
rather than in more goods. Further reductions in the work-
week are needed now, and I think the unions are remiss for not
having moved on this front earlier. However, since all such adjustments have to be slow and gradual, this one in and of itself
can only be a contributory factor. The unions should do more
now to reduce hours and should also put additional penalties
on overtime.

According to the studies we carried on at Columbia University between 1950 and 1960, nine out of ten of the net new jobs
added to the American economy were outside of the private
sector. The not-for-profit sector includes in our calculation direct governmental contractual work even though it goes
through profit-seeking corporations.

Our economy no longer moves—if it ever did—from expansion in the private to expansion in the public sector. There is
more of a circular movement. New York City helps a corporation to build a fair and in the process pays for the construction
of a stadium which it leases back to the Mets, a profit organization. The linkages between the private, the nonprofit, and the
government sectors are less smooth than they ought to be to
permit maximum expansion, and therefore the number of jobs
created through these means is less than it could be.

There are good and bad examples of this fusion of the enterprise systems. In my opinion the outstanding entrepreneur in
the United States in the 1950s was a New York bureaucrat
called Robert Moses. He did more building, created more employment, created more services in that decade than any other
human being in the United States. Yet I am told it takes seven
years for the Board of Education in New York City to get a
school built. If the nonprofit and government sectors of the

economy play such a large part in enterprise, increased employment, I suggest, should be tied to improving their operations.

On another front, there has been some interesting experimentation in the use of industry to accomplish important social ends; e.g., building missiles through governmental contracting, or selling cotton below the market price to domestic manufacturers. It might also be worth-while for the government to experiment with contracts with large or small profit-making organizations willing to use certain kinds of unemployed people. The service sector is where employment potentials loom largest. No substantial number of jobs is likely to be added to manufacturing, and there are very few jobs left in agriculture and mining. The large sector called services offers our hope of expansion, but it is poorly organized. Instead of making missiles, which though necessary are of dubious long-term value, perhaps we can challenge the business community to experiment with the use of people under certain kinds of cost guarantees.

I think it is desirable for Congress to continue on the path it has now opened up for improved education, training, and work orientation for jobless youth. However, the training programs and the antipoverty programs as now constituted will not by themselves assure the employment of all these people. And, as I have said, I do not believe that focusing exclusively on youth unemployment will yield the type and range of social policies necessary for the effective absorption of all unemployed, including youth. Nor do I believe that there are any simple fiscal measures which can move us from the position we are in and the worsening position that I believe we may yet face because of the increased numbers entering the labor force.

I am convinced that there are no hidden answers in the

books of professors or in the desks of bureaucrats, and that there is a considerable amount of social experimentation that has to be entered upon. And the only way I know of to advance social experimentation in this country is to get a public consensus that the costs of experimenting must be borne because the costs of not experimenting are intolerable.

WHICH GOALS FOR THE FUTURE?

by Robert L. Heilbroner

Robert L. Heilbroner is Visiting Professor at the New School for Social Research in New York, where he previously took his Ph.D. The author of *The Worldly Philosophers, The Future as History,* and *The Limits of American Capitalism,* he is now working on a history of the industrialization of America.

LET me give you my impressions—both of what I did hear and of what I didn't at this Symposium.

First, the problem. In the last ten years, we found jobs for about half a million young people from sixteen to twenty-four. Over the next ten years, we have to find jobs for ten times as many, five million. That is the largest single job-finding challenge we have ever faced. The problem consists not of one problem but of two, each one of which I suppose fragments in turn.

The first problem concerns the fortunate component of those five million youths streaming into the labor force. These are young people who come from what are called nice homes, who go through high school, junior college, or college, and then venture into the cold world to find a niche for themselves. Just to take care of those privileged three or four million will be in itself a straining challenge.

Then there is the second problem—the young people who do not come from nice homes, who go out into the world disaffected and stand on street corners in their shiny leather jackets. They constitute a much smaller number than the fortunate ones, but a much larger problem.

Clearly, to mesh all these five million people into the nation's labor force will require the use of both public and private sectors. I have no doubt there are many things that can be done to accelerate the job-offering potential of the private sector, although this is not a matter that can be easily summarized. One can only point in the direction of a large number of specific proposals which must be explored, including incentive systems of various sorts to make private business eager to employ more youths, or measures taken to encourage the establishment of small businesses and to accelerate the rate of economic expansion in general. The fact remains, however, that the main thrust to the challenge of youth unemployment inevitably comes to lodge with the public sector. The private sector—with a little help—may well be able to absorb the "good" youngsters. But only the public sector will be able to find—or make—jobs for the disprivileged ones.

What is needed is for people in Washington and in state capitals and in the cities to spend money or undertake programs on a larger scale and in a somewhat different direction than hitherto if we are to come within any degree of success in absorbing the unprepared young people who will be coming into the labor market. And in trying to use the public sector effectively, we will have to test to the very hilt the flexibility and adaptability of our social system.

I was struck during the conference by an easy use of words that have a symbolic value. I heard the word "revolution" bandied about. I heard one speaker talk easily about "experimentation" in the face of the catastrophe of Mobilization for Youth. I heard another talk with a kind of easy glibness about what can be done with so-called "massive" programs. I fear that words like these often satisfy our yearning for action—without however guiding it very effectively. The one thing that

I am convinced of is that we cannot solve this problem by using easy slogans, but rather by adopting a whole congeries of individual programs which have to be worked out in painful detail.

I want to talk in this regard also about the problem of automation, because this, too, strikes me as one of the mystical words that confuse rather than clarify the issue. Some think the new technology is a problem because it is more labor-displacing than the old technology. I don't think that is the real problem of automation. I don't really believe that computers, dollar for dollar, displace more workers than old-fashioned overhead conveyors. Rather, I would pose the question of automation in an historic context. If we look back fifty years, we can see that there has been a steady invasion of the private economy by technology in various forms. The most startling area, of course, has been agriculture. A quarter of the labor force in this country worked on farms fifty years ago. Today that is down to something like 8 percent.

Now, what happened to all those people who were kicked off the farms by various kinds of machinery? They went to cities to do various things. One of the things they did was to work in the factories. But now if we look at factory employment fifty years ago and today, we find to our amazement that it is about the same size proportionately as it was—about a third of the labor force. Technology has been going into manufacturing as well as into agriculture. In any given plant it has been displacing people, while at the same time it has been creating new kinds of industries, and the two have more or less maintained a balance. The net effect of technology has been to take people off the farms, *through* the manufacturing sector, and out beyond into another sector called the service sector. Fifty years ago less than a quarter of the work force was in the offices, shops, filling stations, restaurants and other locations of service jobs. Today over half are.

Now, what strikes me as extraordinary about the technological revolution is that it is beginning to invade this last sector. Finally we have begun to get machines that sort and file and literally take over the functions of rows of clerks.

If the real impact of automation is the invasion by machinery of this last refuge for employment, then the question is where are these people going to go? The answer is that they are going to go into those kinds of activities where the forces of the market can be at least temporarily kept out—the public sector, where employment does not depend on making a profit but rather on serving a socially-established end. But if this expansion of the service sector is to take place through public expenditure, we are going to have to relearn certain attitudes in this country about the meaning of public activity and public employment. So long as these are regarded as essentially second-rate—so long as the public sector is looked on as a parasitic attachment to the private sector—I do not think we will be able to solve the long-run employment problem well.

And here we come to what is really the crucial question—the matter of goals. One of the things that I missed in this conference was a consideration of this question of goals.

Some people here tended to say that you really could not expect young people to "get with it," to get into the labor force, to try for and hold a job, until you had first "changed society." But this is clearly a counsel of despair. You can't first change society. Rather, the very effort to put alienated young people back into life as, I hope, angry participants—to make them fight for themselves—is changing society. In the short run, the means and the ends are really one. To work at the problem of the poor and the disprivileged, to help the disprivileged come alive to their own situation and work for themselves, *is* both an end and a means, both a goal and a way of reaching that goal.

This difficult task, which is bound to meet with resistance and to have nine-tenths of disappointment for every tenth of achievement, is indeed an end unto itself. So to those who say "change society first," I say, take heart. Just go on doing the dirty work that must be done and you will help bring about the kind of progress that must be had.

But again there is the larger question about longer-term goals. One speaker said, "All right, suppose you make more employment. What is it worth to a man to take a pick and shovel on a public works project? Is this a life? Is this a job in any sense other than a way to hook onto a few necessary dollars per week? In what other direction can society possibly go?" Since nobody had the nerve to answer that question, I will tell you in what other direction society could go. What must be done is to institute in this country more than the present rudiments of economic planning. We talk with a certain degree of complacency about the amount of control we have over our rates of economic growth. But we really do not have anything like effective control over the operation of the economy. I think we *could* have. I think we could coordinate public and private investment programs, so that we would *know* the rate of economic growth and the future flows of economic activity. That is the minimum necessary goal if we are to handle the employment problem with some degree of certainty.

But, even that doesn't yet really come to grips with the question of what kind of life is then led by those who get what is called employment. So I would like to suggest that the next set of goals must be a rolling back of certain kinds of business prerogatives that sully society at the moment. Let me take an obvious one: the roadblock of real estate interests must somehow be overcome, so that the cities can be made habitable, even enjoyable. Then, too, there is the fouling of the cultural air through advertising fallout. That, too, must be controlled if life is not to be just a free-for-all to acquire goods.

After we have cleaned up some of these elements, I think we are going to have to change the level of public information in this country. That is to say, we are going to have to do something about the mechanism through which ordinary people learn about their world. I do not believe we can have a good society so long as there exist media which are allowed to tell outrageous lies, to distort news and to present and dignify violence. The ability of powerful private individuals to give out as *the* word their own word will have to be circumscribed.

I would also hope that the education system will begin to teach some sense of communality. It is extraordinary how little sense of extended family there exists in this nation. I am appalled by the indifference and coldness to misery that one sees among those who are not miserable, and I conclude that it has never been brought home to them how lucky they are and why the unlucky have come to their own miserable condition.

These propositions will certainly not be accomplished tomorrow. I only hold them out as something to look forward to in the next generation. Are they possible of attainment? I waver between optimism and pessimism. If I had to make a guess, I would say that a great deal of adaptation is possible, although I think there are limits.

Where do the limits lie? This is a matter that depends partly on our willingness to test the limits. When you read about "business sentiment" or "military sentiment" or the sentiments of any other established, vested group, you find they are very rarely monolithic views. There is usually a spectrum of views. Thus there is always the chance that a certain amount of movement can be generated. The country we live in today, ugly and heartless though it may be in many ways, is, I think, less ugly and less heartless than it was twenty or thirty years ago.

The question really is whether the rate of growth of heart on the part of those who are privileged can keep pace with the rate of growth of aspirations of those who are not.